TEN
CANADIAN
WRITERS
IN CONTEXT

CHEN   COADY   CRUMMEY   EDWARDS   ENDICOTT   HILL   MAJOR   ROBINSON   SCOFIELD   THÚY

TEN
CANADIAN
WRITERS
IN CONTEXT

THE UNIVERSITY OF ALBERTA PRESS

Marie Carrière, Curtis Gillespie & Jason Purcell, Editors

Published by

The University of Alberta Press
Ring House 2
Edmonton, Alberta, Canada T6G 2E1
www.uap.ualberta.ca

Copyright © 2016 The University of
Alberta Press

LIBRARY AND ARCHIVES CANADA
CATALOGUING IN PUBLICATION

Ten Canadian writers in context / Marie
Carrière, Curtis Gillespie & Jason Purcell,
editors.

(Robert Kroetsch series)
Includes bibliographical references.
Issued in print and electronic formats.
Text in English; some text in French.
ISBN 978-1-77212-141-4 (paperback).—
ISBN 978-1-77212-284-8 (EPUB).—
ISBN 978-1-77212-285-5 (mobipocket).—
ISBN 978-1-77212-286-2 (PDF)

1. Canadian literature (English)—21st
century—History and criticism. 2. Canadian
literature (English)—21st century. 3. Authors,
Canadian (English). 4. Authorship. I. Carrière,
Marie J., 1971–, editor II. Gillespie, Curtis, 1960–,
editor III. Purcell, Jason, 1990–, editor
IV. Series: Robert Kroetsch series

PS8071.5.T45 2016   C810.9'006   C2016-902271-4
C2016-902272-2

First edition, first printing, 2016.
First printed and bound in Canada by Houghton
Boston Printers, Saskatoon, Saskatchewan.
Copyediting and proofreading
by Joanne Muzak.

A volume in the Robert Kroetsch Series.

The University of Alberta Press is committed
to protecting our natural environment. As
part of our efforts, this book is printed on
Enviro Paper: it contains 100% post-consumer
recycled fibres and is acid- and chlorine-free.

The University of Alberta Press gratefully
acknowledges the support received for its
publishing program from the Government of
Canada, the Canada Council for the Arts, and
the Government of Alberta through the Alberta
Media Fund.

Contents

Acknowledgements VII

INTRODUCTION IX
Making Literature, Literature in the Making
by Marie Carrière, Curtis Gillespie & Jason Purcell

1   **YING CHEN** 1
Experiment and Innovation by Julie Rodgers 3
Le Mangeur (excerpt) 10
L'Ingratitude (excerpt) 14

2   **LYNN COADY** 19
a.k.a. The Wit by Maïté Snauwaert 21
The Antagonist (excerpt) 27

3   **MICHAEL CRUMMEY** 37
The Presence of the Past by Jennifer Bowering Delisle 39
Sweetland (excerpt) 46

4   **CATERINA EDWARDS**   57

History Lost in Forgetfulness by Joseph Pivato   59

Finding Rosa: A Mother with Alzheimer's, a Daughter in Search of the Past

(excerpt)   65

5   **MARINA ENDICOTT**   73

Lights and Shadows across the Continent by Daniel Laforest   75

Close to Hugh (excerpt)   81

6   **LAWRENCE HILL**   93

History and the Truth of Fiction by Winfried Siemerling   95

Meet You at the Door (excerpt)   102

7   **ALICE MAJOR**   113

Metaphors, Myths, and the Eye of the Magpie by Don Perkins   115

The Office Tower Tales (excerpt)   122

8   **EDEN ROBINSON**   139

Reading for B'gwus by Kit Dobson   141

The Sasquatch at Home: Traditional Protocols & Modern Storytelling

(excerpt)   147

9   **GREGORY SCOFIELD**   157

kistêyihtamowin êkwa sâkihitowin (Honour and Love) by Angela Van Essen   159

kipocihkân: Poems New & Selected (excerpt)   164

10   **KIM THÚY**   179

A Gentle Power by Pamela V. Sing   181

Ru (excerpt)   189

Essay Contributors   195

Permissions   201

Acknowledgements

THE EDITORS wish to warmly acknowledge the support that the
Faculty of Arts at the University of Alberta has bestowed upon the
Canadian Literature Centre (CLC) since it came into existence in
2006. Dr. Eric Schloss's leadership gift in turn made possible the cre-
ation of the Centre and thus the fruition of this anniversary anthology.
For their enthusiasm from the very start of this process, many spe-
cial thanks to the ten creative authors featured in this anthology:
Ying Chen, Lynn Coady, Michael Crummey, Caterina Edwards, Marina
Endicott, Lawrence Hill, Alice Major, Eden Robinson, Gregory Scofield,
and Kim Thúy. They most generously agreed to share the beauty of
their talent and the power of their words in celebration of the CLC's
tenth anniversary. Our heartfelt appreciation goes out to the ten essay
contributors: Jennifer Bowering Delisle, Kit Dobson, Daniel Laforest,
Don Perkins, Joseph Pivato, Julie Rodgers, Winfried Siemerling, Pamela
Sing, Maïté Snauwaert, and Angela Van Essen. They have worked
diligently and patiently with us throughout this project, and give col-
legiality its true meaning. CLC Director Marie Carrière thanks her
co-editors, Edmonton author, journalist, and magazine editor Curtis
Gillespie, and writer, singer, and composer Jason Purcell, for their dis-
cerning editorial brilliance, their good humour, and their friendship.

Finally, the editors express love and gratitude to their respective families and friends. These individuals know who they are, and without them, there would be no milestones.

Acknowledgements

INTRODUCTION

Making Literature, Literature in the Making

MARIE CARRIÈRE, CURTIS GILLESPIE & JASON PURCELL

IT IS AN EXCITING TIME to engage with the literatures of Canada.IX

Diverse and powerful voices are increasingly writing back to the
national canon, which makes curating an anthology of contempor-
ary Canadian writers a heady and somewhat daunting task. Making
the choices for this collection was not easy, and we could have gone
in many different directions. In the ten years since its inception in
2006, and thanks to the founding gift of Edmonton bibliophile Dr. Eric
Schloss, the Canadian Literature Centre/Centre de littérature cana-
dienne has hosted over fifty authors in its Brown Bag Lunch (BBL)
reading series. Our BBL authors typically appeared on a Wednesday
at noon in the Old Arts Building on the University of Alberta campus,
always in a full room with an audience comprised of students, staff,
and professors, and most especially of Edmonton's remarkably ardent
community of readers, to whom this anthology is warmly dedicated.
The authors featured in this anthology, ten from the ten years of BBL
readings, have not only passed through our doors to share their work
with our audiences, but they now generously contribute to this print
anthology project as well as an ongoing digital project. The authors'
original readings have been recorded live in front of an audience, or
subsequently in the offices of the Canadian Literature Centre, and can
be seen and heard in a digital archive titled *Inside the Bag: Can Lit Alive!*

(edited by Marie Carrière and Jason Purcell). This online scrapbook (abclc.ca/insidethebag/) accompanies the anthology and houses the video and audio recordings, creative bibliographies by Dylan Bateman, our own take on the Proust Questionnaire, and other supplementary materials.

The CLC pursues a uniquely bilingual and multicultural mandate that consists of a three-fold objective of reaching out to students, researchers, and a wider community of readers. This anthology is in part a celebration of that mission. But its wider aim is to represent diverse voices from various races and ethnicities, writing genres, and backgrounds that inhabit Canadian literature today, and to reflect the country's geographical breadth: Michael Crummey from the east coast of Newfoundland; Eden Robinson from the Kitamaat territory on British Columbia's central coast; Kim Thúy from Montréal, Québec; as well as Edmonton authors who exemplify the vibrant literary community of Alberta. This anthology is unique in that it samples not only contemporary writers from different regions and languages, but also of different genres. It features poetry, nonfiction, and fiction, the latter admittedly a favoured genre in this anthology as it has been in the reading series these past ten years. This volume showcases a lived and living Canadian literature from an interlingual and transcultural perspective.

There is no doubt that the making of anthologies, whether large or small, contributes to the construction of literary histories and institutions, just as it responds to these entities. In this collection, we have a literature written in French, in English, and even in Cree. We have purposely reproduced the two Québécois excerpts in their original language, seeking to underline the fact that in Canada and Québec literature is produced, distributed, and read not only in translation (although thankfully it is!), but also in its original French and English. If French–English bilingualism has been deeply entrenched in the work pursued at the Canadian Literature Centre in the past decade, it has not been as part of a mandated colonial ideology extolling Canada as made up of "two founding nations." We have instead chosen to adopt bilingualism as a practice of open dialogue and comparative literary activity. But we need to do more, to foster and promote further the multilingualism—particularly of Canada's Indigenous peoples—that a truly pluralistic society requires. These writers offer a literature that is contemporary, and thus a literature that is still in its own making. While the excerpts in this anthology can only provide us with mere glimpses into these writings, we hope that our selection is attentive and respectful. If the restriction to ten authors mirrors the tenth anniversary of the BBL reading series, it has also allowed us as editors the space to match each literary selection with a critical essay. The selections thus allow readers and students to engage with an introductory assortment of different texts, traditions, regions, and genres for further discovery and study.

As editors, our impulse was not to rely on nationalist tropes or to contribute to the mythologies of a unified nation. It was not to maximize the power anthologies can have to canonize authors and their works or to determine proper ways of reading them. Instead, our goal is to showcase some of the best living talent in Canadian writing today, and to confirm what many of us already know: far from a homogenous, uniform entity, Canada is truly and inherently made up of linguistic and cultural diversities, as E.D. Blodgett and W.H. New have demonstrated in their important literary histories. The writing practices of the ten authors featured in this collection occur in different languages and emerge from various geographical landscapes. But as the following selections demonstrate, it is their writerly locations, or the form and content of their motifs and themes, that are the crux of what distinguishes them: the caveats of familial ties (Ying Chen); the affects of shame (Lynn Coady); the anxiety of cultural loss (Michael Crummey); the tricks of memory (Caterina Edwards); late-life despair, surprise, and comedy (Marina Endicott); the dynamics of race and language (Lawrence Hill); the biting humour of poetic allegory (Alice Major); the ethics of storytelling (Eden Robinson); the sacredness of love (Gregory Scofield); and the perils and gains of exile (Kim Thúy).

Inevitably, the anthologist must grapple with issues of inclusion and exclusion, not to mention a certain amount of hair-pulling and mea culpa. Anthologies spring from choices both within and beyond editors' control. These are determined by a number of limitations such as availability, space, and funding, as well as considerations of genre, racialized identity, gender parity, and, of course, subjective appreciation. As Diana Brydon reminds us, "Anthologies involve choices and they always reveal a bias" (4). Nonetheless, we believe that the scope of our selection is a good step away from mainstream hegemony and a leap forward to a transcultural viewpoint of Indigenous, Anglo-Canadian, and Québécois writing, held here in juxtaposition and, perhaps for certain future readers, potentially in comparison. The literary excerpts that follow are not the only narratives that construct Canada, or what we know about living in the twenty-first century, or about history and time, or about the workings of story, memoir, and poetry. Perhaps, for some or for many, they are not even the most important texts to do these things, considering all that an anthology of ten authors leaves out. Still, they remain crucial as excerpts held in their contextual light by our ten contributing critics. In this collective space, they show what a lived and living literature has to say about the world of the present, the past, and even the future, and how it is the imagination and the possibilities of language that can transform those worlds.

With a student (Purcell), a writer (Gillespie), and a scholar (Carrière) at the editorial helm, this project is a three-way endeavour highly representative of the Canadian Literature Centre's overarching mission to bring together teaching, writing, and research to foster and promote the literature of this country. The CLC is a research centre whose mandate focuses on both scholarly and literary outreach, giving the critical component of this anthology a symbolic and more importantly a pedagogical purpose. The essays herein play a fundamental role in our attempt to avoid another homogenizing tendency of anthologies: the decontextualization of a work's form and content through its selection and organization in a single space. The essays that supplement each literary excerpt are not written as model readings or student guides. They do not form a collection of essays about literary movements, schools of writing, critical terminology, or academic debate. The essays intend a generalized, though succinct and specific, perspective on the writing, a critical appreciation that addresses our ten authors' preoccupations and practices. We as editors have asked our critics to circumvent close reading and instead provide a point of entry into the author's work and its aesthetic, social, and thematic context. Each in their own voice, the ten critics combine contextual information, accessible critical language, theoretical perspectives, and literary analysis that map out how a writer's texts might be read by informed readers outside the academy as well as taught within universities. This anthology is therefore intended as a resource for teachers and students (of advanced secondary school English and university programs) as well as the general reader of Canadian literature in English and in French. The literary selections and critical essays will be of interest not only to teachers and students of Canadian literature, but to engaged readers who want to know how to perform a critical reading of these authors' work.

Our hope is that this anthology will not only begin to showcase the thrilling range and talent of this country's literature—which the Canadian Literature Centre has worked hard to promote these past ten years—but to allow the levelling of differences, the productive comparison, and the appreciation of the literary work featured in this collection. We seek to prompt a rich reading and a deeper understanding of the selected authors' work, here in these pages, and certainly beyond them.

Edmonton, February 2016

Works Cited

Blodgett, E.D. *Five-Part Invention: A History of Literary History in Canada.* Toronto: University of Toronto Press, 2003. Print.

Brydon, Diana. "Postcolonial Pedagogy and Curricular Reform." Keynote Address at Red Deer College, Alberta, 1997. Web. 21 May 2015.

New, W.H. *A History of Canadian Literature.* 2nd ed. Kingston and Montréal: McGill-Queen's University Press, 2003. Print.

YING CHEN is a novelist, short story writer, essayist, poet, and translator, often identified with a second wave of *écriture migrante* (migrant writing) in Québec. However, she has always resisted fixed positions; despite living and writing between geographic and linguistic locations, Chen evades labels that would make her representative of the immigrant experience. She was born in Shanghai, China, in 1961. In 1983, she earned a degree in French language and literature from Fudan University and worked as an interpreter and translator, mastering English, Mandarin, Japanese, and Russian. She moved to Montréal in 1989 to attend McGill University, earning a master's degree in creative writing in 1991, and now divides her time between British Columbia and France. Chen's writing career began in the early 1990s when she began to write and publish in French, a decision that she considers an act of rebellion against the formal education she received in China during the Cultural Revolution. Inspired by her grandmother's life and focused on memory and female subservience, her first novel, *La Mémoire de l'eau* (Leméac, 1992), examines four generations of women in modern China through a historical lens. Her second novel, *Les Lettres chinoises* (Leméac, 1993), is an epistolary novel composed of the correspondence between two lovers, one of whom lives in China and the other in Québec. Her third novel,

L'Ingratitude (Leméac, 1995), marked a stylistic turn that has come to characterize the rest of Chen's oeuvre. Through a bare but highly affective form, *L'Ingratitude* depicts a young woman who violently resists conventional cultural obedience exemplified by her mother; the book won the Prix Québec-Paris, the Prix de Libraires du Québec from the Association of Québec booksellers, and the Elle Québec Magazine Readers' Prize. The novel was also nominated for the Governor General's Award for French-language fiction and the prestigious Prix Fémina in 1995. Carol Volk translated *L'Ingratitude* into English as *Ingratitude* (Douglas & McIntyre, 1998), and it has also been translated into Chinese, Italian, Spanish, and Serbian. Her next novel, *Immobile* (Boréal, 1998), won the Prix Alfred-DesRochers de l'Association des auteurs des Cantons-de-l'Est in 1999. A prolific, widely read, and highly original contemporary writer, Chen has also published *Le Champ dans la mer* (Boréal, 2002), *Querelle d'un squelette avec son double* (Boréal, 2003), the essay collection *Quatre mille marches* (Boréal, 2004), *Le Mangeur (Boréal, 2006), Un Enfant à ma porte* (Boréal, 2008), *Espèces* (Boréal, 2010), *La Rive est loin* (Boréal, 2013), and *La Lenteur des montagnes* (Boréal, 2014). In 2002, Chen was made chevalière des Arts et des Lettres by the French government, and her work has been the object of much academic research. In spring 2009, she was Shadbolt fellow in the French Department of Simon Fraser University. Ying Chen visited the Canadian Literature Centre to deliver her Brown Bag Lunch reading on September 16, 2015.

1

YING CHEN

Experiment and Innovation

YING CHEN has experimented with a variety of literary genres
including the essay, poetry, short stories, translation, and theatre, but
she has risen to prominence primarily as a novelist. Her novels can be
roughly divided into two strands, both of which are represented in this
anthology. The first, a series of three early texts, comprises *La Mémoire
de l'eau* (1992), *Les Lettres chinoises* (1993), and *L'Ingratitude* (1995), which,
despite their loosely shared Chinese settings, constitute stand-alone
novels for the most part. The second and more cohesive cycle opens
with *Immobile* (1998) and concludes with *La Rive est loin* (2013), with
Le Champ dans la mer (2002), *Querelle d'un squelette avec son double* (2003),
Le Mangeur (2006), *Un Enfant à ma porte* (2009), and *Espèces* (2010), filling
the fifteen-year interval and giving rise to a substantial series of seven
novels in total. As critic Martine-Emmanuelle Lapointe notes, what
distinguishes the second cycle from the first is the increasing difficulty
of ascribing to the texts not only a specific geographical location but a
linear time frame (134). The lack of a fixed setting and time sequence is,
however, not the sole reason for grouping these novels into a cycle;
there is substantial thematic overlap and they are also linked by the
recurrence in each text of the same unnamed protagonist who is mar-
ried to an archaeologist known only as A.

For Émile Talbot, this fissure or divergence in Chen's novel-length fiction indicates a shift in her artistic vision announced in *L'Ingratitude* but which comes to full fruition in the second series and is characterized by an increased preference for the symbolic. It is a split that Chen herself acknowledges in *Quatre mille marches* (2004) and restates in her most recent publication *La Lenteur des montagnes* (2014). Both of these texts, the former a series of short essays and the latter constructed as a letter of sorts to her son, offer key insights into the nature of Chen's fiction and the issues with which it is concerned. In *Quatre mille marches*, Chen alludes to what she considers to be the second series, describing it as "un ensemble romanesque...ayant comme personage central une femme de nature ambiguë qui raconte ses vicissitudes désencadrées du temps et de l'espace" (97; "a fictional ensemble...having as a central character a woman of ambiguous nature who relates frameless vicissitudes of time and space"), and goes on to highlight the commonalities between the novels pertaining to this cycle (99). In *La Lenteur des montagnes*, there are several references to a second phase of writing. Indeed, Chen herself employs the word "series" to refer to her cohort of "romans ténébreux sur le temps, l'espace et les instincts" (26; "gloomy novels on time, space and instincts") and delineates a rupture between the pre-1995 and post-1995 novels with *L'Ingratitude* serving as the hinge between the two cycles (86).

Given Chen's prolific literary output and willingness to experiment with style, it is not surprising that there are many critical approaches to her work. Chen's fiction has garnered attention for its discussion of, inter alia, the migrant experience; the condition of women; the question of human existence; the complex politics of identity; the ambiguous bonds of familial and conjugal relations; and the unstable nature of time, space, and movement. For the most part, the point of view of Chen's fiction is female. There are only two instances in Chen's oeuvre where we find a first-person male narrator: *Lettres chinoises* (from the first series) where we have access to Juan's thoughts, and the final novel of the second series, *La Rive est loin*, where Chen gives a voice to the otherwise silent male character of A. This preference for a female narrator in addition to the choice of societal institutions that undergo critique in Chen's writing (such as marriage and motherhood) has, understandably, led a number of scholars such as Saint-Martin, Porret, and Rodgers to interpret the author's work from the angle of feminist theory despite the author's own endeavours to reject critical labels and distance herself from any specific politics in her fiction: "Je n'ai aucun message à livrer...Je ne m'adresse pas au monde extérieur, mais m'achemine vers l'intérieur" (*Quatre mille marches* 60; "I have no message to deliver...I do not address the external world but move toward the internal"). In *Quatre mille marches,* Chen expresses frustration at being reduced to her origins and exhibited as a *porte-parole* for the Chinese migrant (41), a point reiterated in *La Lenteur des montagnes*: "J'ai décidé que je ne peux plus me tenir à quoi que ce soit de local, que je bois l'eau de toutes les mers, que je respire l'air de l'univers, que je reçois l'enseignement des maîtres de tous les temps sans être disciple d'aucun" (13-14; "I have decided that I can no longer hold myself to anything local, that I drink the water of all the seas, that I breathe the air of the universe, that I receive the teaching of masters of all times without being anyone's disciple"). For Chen, the primary aim of writing is the pursuit of clarity and simplicity (24) and, one could posit, a holism that exceeds the boundaries of place and time. Boundaries and categories are, therefore, depicted in Chen's fiction as limiting and regressive and a more expansive and outward-bound, nomadic vision of the world is favoured.

A central preoccupation running through Chen's fiction is that of existence and, conjointly, identity, be that as a migrant, a woman, a mother, a daughter, a wife, or a writer. However, although a consistent trope in Chen's novels, little about the nature of identity is presented to the reader. On the contrary, identity for Chen is not fixed or defined, but is, rather, a creation forever in flux. Chen is interested in identity more as a process than as a product, proclaiming in *Quatre milles marches* that "l'important est de continuer à marcher et non d'arriver réellement" (32; "what matters is to continue walking rather than to really arrive"). Identity, for Chen, is malleable and multiple. As a result, the recurring unnamed female protagonist of the second cycle does not live one single, traceable, measurable life but instead flits back and forth between past and present, is reincarnated, experiences doubling, and even inhabits more than one species. (For example, she becomes a cat in *Espèces*). Chen destabilizes the fixedness of start and end points, origins and destinations, by favouring the liminal and positioning her protagonist between worlds, between time zones, between bodies, between desires. Chen extends this relentless liminality—a source of both internal conflict and empowerment for the protagonist—to the experience of the migrant and the writer, which reflects her own personal trajectory. In *La Lenteur des montagnes* she states, "La migration et l'écriture sont pour moi une seule et même expérience: descendre dans un tunnel en espérant effectuer une traversée, comprendre que, finalement, il n'y aura pas de traversée, que le tunnel est déjà la destination, que ma vie entière s'écoulera ici" (54; "Migration and writing are for me the one and the same experience: to go down a tunnel hoping to make a crossing, to understand that, finally, there will be no crossing, that the tunnel is already the destination, that my entire life will be spent here"). Such musings on liminality and unstable identities give rise to a reflection of difference or otherness. The recurring anonymous female protagonist is haunted by a sense of otherness that she frequently terms her "fâcheuse condition" (*Le champ dans la mer* 8; "unsettling condition"). Those around her, particularly her husband, try to tame her, correct her, and render her alterity less obvious. The protagonist seems torn between an urge to belong and a determination to resist assimilation, a trait that is characteristic of migrancy but could also be explained by her female otherness within a patriarchal society. Chen's fiction, however, portrays difference as something that should be respected and valorized rather than feared, for, after all, as the Grandmother proclaims in *La Mémoire de l'eau*, "l'odeur des eaux mortes [est] partout la même" (115; "the odour of dead waters is the same everywhere").

The two extracts that the author has selected for inclusion here exemplify many of the tropes and themes that characterize her work as a whole. *L'Ingratitude*, strictly speaking, constitutes the final novel of the looser first cycle but, as previously stated, announces the changes that are to come in the second series of texts of which *Le Mangeur* is the fourth. *L'Ingratitude* contains forward references to *Le Mangeur* with the mention of the fish: this is an example of intratextuality, internal referencing within a single body of work, and it is a narrative technique Chen employs in almost all of her novels, adding to the sense of collapsing boundaries that permeates her writing.

Both excerpts depict the parent-child relationship (mother and daughter in the case of *L'Ingratitude* and father and daughter in *Le Mangeur*). Ancestral lineage is a prominent theme in Chen's oeuvre. The protagonist seeks to escape her origins through suicide (albeit failed) in *L'Ingratitude*, but openly embraces a return to origins through the ingestion scene in *Le Mangeur* depicted here. This problematic parent-child relationship, which recurs throughout Chen's writing, serves as a metaphor for the migrant experience and the push and pull that her characters often suffer, drawn towards a new life but simultaneously remaining attached to the old one. Both excerpts also allude to the disintegration of time and memory characteristic of Chen's work as well as the inversion of the life/death dichotomy. Death, in Chen's fiction, is not necessarily finite but merely another stage in a life cycle that has the potential to continue well beyond it. A further hierarchy challenged by Chen in her fiction, and that appears in these extracts through the references to the fish and the bird, is that of the human/animal binary. Rather than privilege the human over the animal, Chen often connects her protagonist to a non-human state, thus displacing anthropocentrism, that is, the belief in the exclusive dominance of the human, and evoking a more dynamic transpecies relationality. Thus, in Chen's fiction, human characters resemble animals—for example, the father's aquatic condition in *Le Mangeur* and the female protagonist's identification with the silkworm in *Un Enfant à ma porte*. This human-animal co-extensivity is pushed even further in *Espèces* with the female protagonist's feline physical metamorphosis, during which she retains human psychological aspects.

Ying Chen is one of the most experimental and radical Canadian writers of the twenty-first century. Deceptively simplistic, her novels dismantle societal systems and unsettle reader expectations on a number of levels. Her narratives contain several layers and intersect with each other thus giving rise to a multitude of possible interpretations. Her definition of subjecthood as unstable, moveable, and attached to multiple communities is one that explodes the normative and conservative vision of the unified, self-contained individual. In fact, the emphasis on plurality in Chen's work renders her a writer very much of our time. With its rapid technological advances, increasing globalization, and hybridization of identity, the twenty-first century is one where, as Chen herself observes, "le changement est une loi absolue dans un monde sans absolu" (*La Lenteur de Montagnes* 12; "change is an absolute law in a world without absolutes"). Chen's fiction, by encouraging us to think outside established parameters, can therefore help us to make sense of our complex and constantly mutating postmodern realities. In fact, one could even posit that Chen's vision of existence is powerfully ecosophical (merging ecology and philosophy). Chen imagines a more ethical future where the monolithism of classical humanism is disrupted and a new in-between subject that is connected to various temporal, physical, and environmental forces can flourish.

Works Cited

Chen, Ying. *Le Champ dans la mer*. Paris: Seuil, 2002. Print.

———. *Un Enfant à ma porte*. Paris: Seuil, 2009. Print.

———. *Espèces*. Paris: Seuil, 2010. Print.

———. *Immobile*. Arles: Actes Sud, 1998. Print.

———. *L'Ingratitude*. Montréal: Leméac, 1995. Print.

———. *La Lenteur des montagnes*. Montréal: Boréal, 2014. Print.

———. *Les Lettres chinoises*. Montréal: Leméac, 1993. Print.

———. *Le Mangeur*. Paris: Seuil, 2006. Print.

———. *La Mémoire de l'eau*. Leméac: Montréal, 1992. Print.

———. *Quatre mille marches*. Paris: Seuil, 2004. Print.

———. *Querelle d'un squelette avec son double*. Paris: Seuil, 2003. Print.

———. *La Rive est loin*. Paris: Seuil, 2013. Print.

Lapointe, Martine-Emmanuelle. "Le mort n'est jamais mort: Emprise des origines et conceptions de la mémoire dans l'œuvre de Ying Chen." *Voix et Images* 29.2 (2004): 131-14. Print.

Porret, Véronique. "La féminité est-elle subversive ? D'une psychanalyste français à une psychanalyse chinoise." 2007. Web.

Rodgers, Julie. "Comment peut-on être *moi* quand on est *Mère*? Une étude de la maternité dans *Un enfant à ma porte* (2009) de Ying Chen." *International Journal of Canadian Studies* 45/46 (2012): 403-16. Print.

Saint-Martin, Lori. "Infanticide, Suicide, Matricide, and Mother-Daughter Love: Suzanne Jacob's *L'obéissance* and Ying Chen's *L'Ingratitude*." *Canadian Literature* 169 (2001): 60-83. Print.

Talbot, Emile. "Rewriting *Les Lettres chinoises*: The Poetics of Erasure." *Québec Studies* 36 (2003/2004): 83-91. Print.

Le Mangeur (excerpt)

SI EN CET APRÈS-MIDI, pendant un instant, je m'étais sentie confrontée à une difficulté de choix, je n'aurais pas hésité longtemps entre les bras de mon ami et le ventre de mon père. J'avais, parmi toutes les émotions qu'on puisse éprouver face à la mort, un souhait qui n'était même pas formulé, qui restait au fond de moi et n'avait pas encore pu monter à la surface en forme de pensée. Je souhaitais, sans le savoir, que tout soit terminé avant l'heure du rendez-vous, que mon ami arrive trop tard pour une raison ou une autre devant notre maison redevenue calme, qu'ainsi exclu à jamais il ne s'attarde pas sous notre fenêtre peu accueillante et laisse mon père tranquille, qu'il s'en aille comme si de rien n'était, comme si je n'avais jamais existé.

Cependant, au moment où je fus brusquement soulevée et vite transportée jusque dans la gorge de mon père, en regardant sans tristesse ni frayeur l'intérieur de mon père où bougeaient les veines et la chair rouge, je ne pus m'empêcher d'éprouver un dégoût envers cette bourdonnante vie interne que mon père considérait comme l'essence de la peinture. Je ressentis un bref regret du rendez-vous manqué, me reprochai de ne pas aimer assez mon ami, de manquer de courage pour me lancer dans un avenir qui m'était maintenant à jamais fermé, suspendu dans l'air frais du dehors, loin de toute vibration corporelle — mon ami et moi nous n'avions pas encore eu de contact physique. Je glissai la tête en bas dans un des tubes paternels, au bout duquel je serais, selon mon père, doucement dissoute et assimilée. Au cours de ma descente vers l'intérieur d'un corps si vibrant et si vrai, que je n'avais pas pu imaginer, devant cette révélation, je commençai à me blâmer de la sécheresse de mon corps et de mon esprit du temps où je vivais encore. J'attribuais tout cela à un excès d'amour-propre, à la plus grande avarice qui consistait à ne pas donner l'amour, à ne pas se donner à un autre. Supposons que mon ami arrive à temps et commence sans tarder à sauver, à ouvrir le ventre de mon père, en ce moment affaibli par le volume du repas, ressemblant à une femme enceinte, que pourrait-il bien se passer? Serais-je vraiment capable d'en sortir intacte et de vivre désormais tel un nouveau-né, loin de mon père, sans mémoire?

| Des années plus tard, peut-être, en vivant avec A. une vie quotidienne semée de heurts, j'ai appris que, faute de porter les mêmes gènes que lui, je n'entrerais jamais dans son livret familial, que je ne serais jamais « des leurs » malgré notre alliance par le mariage. Je crois alors mieux comprendre mon père, son affection exclusive pour moi, son étroitesse, son retrait, ses convictions quant à l'insurmontable obstacle à ce qu'on appelle la solidarité pure et simple, le rapprochement désintéressé entre des êtres différents. Aujourd'hui, je n'ai plus honte de mon choix. Je ne regrette rien, ni de sortir du temps de mon père ni de perdre mon ami que je n'ai jamais vraiment connu. À l'exception de mon père avec qui je partageais l'héritage de l'aïeule, la même maladie incurable, la même source malsaine, je ne pourrais jamais gagner le cœur de personne, dans ma condition, en étant ce que je suis. De cela je fais une loi.

| En fait, en rentrant « à la maison », dans le corps même de mon père, en descendant vers ma source qui pourtant me répugnait, instinctivement je suivais cette loi. À ma disparition, la douleur que mon ami éprouverait probablement ne dépasserait pas, en intensité et en profondeur, celle d'un père désolé. J'en étais persuadée. Mon ami encore très jeune ne manquerait pas de trouver une consolation. Il se détournerait, en bas de ma fenêtre, vers le chemin qui s'étendait loin devant

lui, où dans sa soudaine solitude il lui serait possible de rencontrer aussitôt une jeune fille non moins intéressante que moi. Il devait courir, aimer au maximum, vivre à fond comme on dit, comme on l'espère. Bientôt d'autres femmes combleraient son existence, le reproduiraient même, sans précision toutefois, en lui donnant des enfants. Or j'étais la seule pour mon père. Il n'aurait pas d'autres enfants. Il n'en voudrait pas. Et nous ne serions plus malades en quittant ensemble ce monde qui ne nous convenait pas. Ainsi, mourir de l'imbécile langueur dans les bras d'un bien-aimé ne vaut pas toujours mieux que de périr dans la boue de son créateur, en toute simplicité, confiance et... liberté.

J'y plongeai donc, dans cette boue, la tête la première. Contente de redevenir un tas de chair sans forme, à l'abri de toute souffrance, du danger de ressembler trop à mon père, d'être trop différente des autres, de me transformer en un monstre, de ne pas être aimée, de devenir une curiosité dans le monde où j'étais. Plus envie ni prétention de tacher les toiles. Rien à peindre lorsque tout devenait couleur et liquide. Plus rien à représenter le jour où une faim triompha sur un amour. Le personnage de mon père semblait alors vivant, il était sorti de sa toile. Je pensais que la toile, devenue alors vide et fade, était à jeter.

La digestion pourrait se faire tranquillement, sans le moindre risque d'allergie, parce que les organes de mon père reconnaîtraient les tissus et d'autres éléments de moi. Je devais être facilement assimilable. L'épicière n'aurait pas imaginé cela. Aucune trace pour encourager une enquête judiciaire sérieuse. Mon père aurait maintenant suffisamment d'énergie, je supposais, pour plusieurs jours. Ensuite, quand il retrouverait la paix intérieure, il irait comme d'habitude chez les vendeurs de viande. Il annoncerait ma disparition calmement. Les vendeurs souhaiteraient qu'il puisse se tirer de cette tragédie. Ils seraient tous ruinés si jamais mon père allait en prison. Quand il ferait beau, il pourrait pêcher dans la rivière, par plaisir mais aussi pour économiser. Car depuis quelque temps les dépenses pour la nourriture étaient devenues l'un de mes soucis importants. J'étais contente de l'utilité de mon corps, de ma mort. Si mon ami arrivait en ce moment, du haut de notre fenêtre mon père n'aurait qu'à secouer la tête, et l'autre s'en irait, résigné et raisonnable, n'ayant pas l'intention de contrarier la volonté d'un père, ne trouvant pas de raison d'insister puisqu'il connaissait encore très peu mon sentiment envers lui. En route, il essayerait de se rappeler les paroles et les sourires échangés rapidement entre nous lorsqu'on était encore à la même école. Les souvenirs seraient plutôt minces. Et il s'interrogerait sur le fondement même de ce rendez-vous.

L'Ingratitude (excerpt)

SANS SEIGNEUR NILOU, je ne sais pas où me diriger. Je ne reconnais plus la gauche ni la droite, plus le haut ni le bas. Plus de direction. Autrefois, je cherchais une direction. Je voulais faire des choix. Je voulais choisir une mère, ou du moins la faire changer à mon gré. Choisir mon homme. Choisir entre la vie et la mort ainsi que la façon de mourir. Maintenant, en même temps que de mon corps, je suis déchargée de tous ces choix qui jadis m'ont causé tant de chagrins et qui maintenant sont devenus insignifiants comme la poudre de ma chair.

| Les gens vont et viennent en émettant une fumée épaisse qui me sépare d'eux. Je vois mal ce qui les pousse à s'agiter. Maman continue à manger, à remuer tantôt ses lèvres, tantôt ses membres et à dormir. Elle prononce des choses que je comprends à peine. J'ai l'impression qu'elle parle de moi. Déjà, elle paraît moins triste. Je pense que même si j'avais réussi mon suicide, je n'aurais pu la faire souffrir davantage. D'ailleurs, tout cela n'a plus d'importance. Ma haine a brûlé dans le four où on a lancé mon corps. Maman a dans son air cette candeur propre aux vivants qui croient que la mort n'est qu'un accident. Des vagues de poussière, sortant des ruines des ancêtres et portant des générations de déchets, roulent autour d'elle et blanchissent ses cheveux sans qu'elle

s'en rende compte. Je découvre pour la première fois que maman est en fait aussi innocente et vulnérable comme les autres. Elle vit encore. Elle respecte ses horaires. Elle marche d'un pas héroïque et s'assoit comme une montagne. Elle dort d'un sommeil profond. Elle ignore la poussière en train de la remplir, elle et tout ce qui l'entoure. Lorsque la poussière deviendra trop épaisse, l'eau de la mer envahira la ville et les corps seront nettoyés. Je vois maman dans le ventre d'un poisson. Et je me vois dans le ventre de maman. Nous avons mangé tant de poissons. Maman me paraît maintenant moins solide. Je l'aime mieux ainsi. J'aurais voulu le lui dire. Mais c'est trop tard. De toute façon, cela vaut mieux ainsi.

Chun est enfin sorti avec une jeune fille. Je les vois marcher côte à côte dans cette rue où il m'a poursuivie furieusement. Leurs manches se frôlent. Il semble vouloir éviter le bras très charnu de sa copine, son souvenir de moi étant encore présent. Mais lui, elle et moi, nous savons tous qu'il va prendre ce bras bientôt, pour on ne sait pas encore combien de saisons. Le soleil brillait dans leurs yeux. Et ils sourient. C'est, me semble-t-il, le plus beau couple que j'aie jamais vu.

Il y en a qui descendent vite la pente. Papa reste de plus en plus dans son lit. Grand-mère commence à perdre ses cheveux, sa mémoire et ses dents. Oncle Pan déménage à l'hôpital où des femmes énormes attendent leur bébé. Et voilà que maman a acheté un jeune oiseau et l'a mis dans une cage suspendue sous la fenêtre. Elle lui parle quelquefois. Une tendresse nouvelle s'épanouit sur son visage en y effaçant une tristesse usée. Elle lèche sa plaie, se soigne bravement. Elle continue à aimer à sa façon. Elle se met à éduquer et à discipliner son oiseau, pour se réconforter de son échec antérieur, se préparer un avenir quelconque, léguer son patrimoine et assurer une continuité à sa vie. Personne à sa place ne pourrait agir autrement. Il faut boucler la boucle tant bien que mal. Ce qu'elle est en train de faire me paraît très émouvant.

Or, ce n'est peut-être pas elle, cette femme à côté d'une cage d'oiseau. Je ne suis pas très sûre de la reconnaître. Je commence à perdre la vue, à mélanger les proches et les étrangers, les gens et les bêtes, les êtres et les choses. D'ailleurs, je ne peux plus distinguer aujourd'hui d'hier. Je ne vois pas de demain. Je me rends compte alors que je suis bel et bien morte. Quand on est vivant, on évalue le temps. On compte les années, les saisons, les journées et les secondes. Rien n'échappe à ce calcul. Même la lumière et le sable ont un âge. De cette façon, on se donne l'impression de posséder un nombre considérable de saisons, encore plus de journées et enfin d'innombrables secondes. On s'assure d'avoir le temps de tout faire, de s'aimer et de se haïr, de tout construire et de tout démolir. Pour participer à tout cela, il faut avoir un corps vivant. Alors je suis mise à la porte. Quel soulagement enfin de se trouver hors de ce jeu interminable, d'être à l'abri du temps, de ce bouillonnement rythmé des amours et des rancœurs, des plaisirs et des ennuis, des naissances et des morts, des parents et des enfants... Mais comment connaître ce bonheur nouveau, intemporel et vide, sans avoir vécu à l'intérieur du temps, sans avoir étouffé dans sa plénitude? Comment éprouver la joie glaciale de l'étranger sans avoir déjà eu une patrie? Et enfin, comment apprendre à se débarrasser d'une mère sans être jamais né? Être l'enfant d'une femme est donc une chance qui permet de connaître le bonheur de ne pas l'être. Une chance à laquelle on doit beaucoup de gratitude.

Je me presse de contempler cette ville devenue de plus en plus floue, lointaine et incompréhensible. Ces choses pourtant familières, rues et rivière, mères et rats, flottent autour de moi en se décomposant et en changeant de couleur. Et moi aussi, je flotte. Je vais très loin. Pour la première et la dernière fois, sans doute, j'écoute les murmures des Alpes, je touche la chaleur du Sahara, je bois les eaux amères du Pacifique. Tout paraît très beau quand il n'y a plus de choix à faire, quand on aime sans objet, quand Seigneur Nilou ne vient pas, quand on n'a plus de destin.

J'entends encore des voix méfiantes ou sympathiques qui parlent de moi, puisque dans le cimetière, la boîte qui enferme une partie des cendres de mon corps est encore à sa place, encore bien rangée, alors que certaines boîtes sont déjà en désordre ou perdues. La lumière envahit tout, ivre et triomphante. Le paysage recule, rétrécit et s'efface. Je ne vois plus rien. Je ne vois pas maman. Je n'ai plus personne, ni maman ni Seigneur Nilou. Mon souvenir de maman se fond dans cette lumière

uniforme. Ma mémoire s'évapore ainsi que le nuage qui me porte.
À travers le brouillard de cette mémoire, me parvient, comme une
lamentation enchantée, une dernière voix humaine, le cri d'un nour-
risson peut-être :

Maman!

LYNN COADY's work has found much-deserved critical and public acclaim. Born in 1970 in Port Hawkesbury, Nova Scotia, Coady lived on Cape Breton Island until she moved to Ottawa to attend Carleton University in 1988. Coady began her undergraduate education in journalism but finished with a bachelor of arts in English and philosophy. She then went to Fredericton, New Brunswick, where she wrote her first play and began her first novel, working odd jobs while focusing on her writing. In 1996, she moved to Vancouver to attend the University of British Columbia, where she earned a master of fine arts degree in creative writing. It was at this point in her life that Coady wrote her first novel, *Strange Heaven* (Goose Lane Editions, 1998, 2010). The novel was nominated for the 1998 Governor General's Award for English-language fiction, marking Coady's first step into Canada's literary spotlight. She was then awarded the Canadian Authors Association/Air Canada Award for Canada's most promising writer under thirty. She was also awarded the Dartmouth Book Award for Fiction and the 1999 Atlantic Bookseller's Choice Award. Coady's second book, a collection of short stories called *Play the Monster Blind* (Doubleday, 2000), was a national bestseller and a *Globe and Mail* "Best Book" in 2000. In 2001, the collection won the Canadian Authors Association's Jubilee Award for Short Stories. *Play the Monster Blind* was also shortlisted for the 2000 Rogers Writers' Trust Fiction Prize and the

Stephen Leacock Award for Humour. Coady followed the success of this collection with her second novel *Saints of Big Harbour* (Doubleday, 2002), which was also a *Globe and Mail* "Best Book" in 2002. In 2005, Coady was recognized by the Canada Council with the Victor Martyn Lynch-Staunton Award for an artist in mid-career. Coady then published *Mean Boy* (Doubleday, 2006), winning the Writers' Guild of Alberta's Georges Bugnet Award for Fiction in 2007, and securing yet another "Best Book" nod from the *Globe and Mail*. Coady followed *Mean Boy* with *The Antagonist* (House of Anansi Press, 2011), which won the 2012 Georges Bugnet Award for Fiction and was shortlisted for the 2011 Scotiabank Giller Prize. Coady's most recent book, *Hellgoing* (House of Anansi Press, 2013), a collection of short stories, was awarded the 2013 Scotiabank Giller Prize and was shortlisted for the Rogers Writers' Trust Fiction Prize. *Hellgoing* was also selected as an Amazon.ca Best Book and as one of the *Globe and Mail's* Top 10 Books of 2013.

A common thread of wry humour runs throughout Coady's fiction, through which she explores the absurdities and hypocrisies of life in Maritime Canada. Not only a successful fiction writer, Coady is also a talented journalist whose work has been featured in publications such as *Saturday Night* and *This Magazine*. Coady was also senior writer and editor at *Adbusters*, based in Vancouver, and with Curtis Gillespie she co-founded *Eighteen Bridges*, published in Edmonton by the Canadian Literature Centre. Coady has edited several anthologies, including, among others, *The Journey Prize Stories 20: The Best of Canada's New Writers* (Emblem, McClelland & Stewart, 2008) with Heather O'Neill and Neil Smith. Coady now also writes for television, with credits including the internationally successful *Orphan Black* (Temple Street Productions, 2013) and *Sensitive Skin* (Rhombus Media, Baby Cow Productions, 2014). On April 13, 2015, Coady delivered the clc Kreisel Lecture, *Who Needs Books? Reading in the Digital Age*. The lecture was broadcast on cbc Radio One *Ideas* as "The Monster at the End," and is published in the clc Kreisel Lecture Series by the University of Alberta Press and the Canadian Literature Centre (2016). Coady now lives in Toronto. She visited the Canadian Literature Centre for her Brown Bag Lunch reading on October 6, 2010.

2

LYNN COADY A.K.A. THE WIT

MAÏTÉ SNAUWAERT

THE CHARACTERS that populate Lynn Coady's novels and short stories are teenagers caught in the difficulty of college years or the process of entering adulthood, young and not-so-young men and women struggling with disillusion and grief, and self-deprecating narrators confined to desolate places. If these dark and humorous creatures occasionally rejoice with their fellow heavy drinkers, they also become, when they have the writer's streak in them, big fans of the solitary teapot. Their divine comedy is played out in the remotest locales of Canada, from one ocean to the other but especially in the Maritimes, on faraway islands and in small towns whose names are unknown to outsiders, where the place of gathering is the fast-food parking lot, and both unexpected and ordinary tension seeps out of the dullness. These characters live, and occasionally even evolve, in the midst of repressed hysterical families, governed as much by religion as by a cementing mentality unequipped to soothe their angst. What saves them (though not always) from these ancestors, their peers, themselves, and the bleakness of their surroundings is their acute lucidity, coarse language, and piquant wit. And it is also their reflective minds, which are rarely broad enough to allow self-indulgence but usually wide enough to make them want to flee.

These are the people Coady deploys to get at the heart of one of her main themes, which is the tragic fantasy of escape from small-town Maritime poverty and parochialism. Such a fantasy embodies a deeper sense of existential unease. In this regard, the uneventful Maritime—and perhaps to a larger extent Canadian—scene, with its low-key features, provides a perfect setting to stage the profound emotional and physical malaise that is at the heart of Lynn Coady's universe.

The Inner Grip

Lynn Coady is the portrait artist of existential anxiety. She is particularly adept at describing intermediate ages—boy into man (*Mean Boy*), girl into woman (*Strange Heaven*)—and the muddy emergence of a sense of self. Her coming-of-age stories let us hear the inner voice of her characters' turmoil, as they try to navigate the confusing transitions between the end of childhood and the beginning of adulthood, or the blurred line marking the end of immaturity and the dawn of responsibility. Coady masters the first-person narrative, the inner voice, the thoughts of self-flagellation (as in *The Antagonist*). She excels at portraying the deep, inescapable feeling of guilt, the shame so intensely interwoven in the fabric of one's personality. We meet her characters as they struggle to become fully-fledged individuals, distinct from parental, gender, and social expectations, grappling with abortions literal and symbolic, and facing their obvious, inherited inability to accept themselves.

The brute is a favourite character, desperately trying to assert his way between virility and brutality, force and strength, pure physical manpower and moral fortitude, the former regarded as a curse rather than a blessing. "He is so *big*, thought Sara. He could kill me" (*Hellgoing* 127). Bordering on the bigger-than-life or even the monstrous, the males' heaviness obfuscates their actual sensitivity, and this is echoed in their accounts of self-loathing. The characters' physique is an embodiment of the shame bestowed on their sense of self, but also a comical reminder that whatever personal crisis they might have fancied themselves living is really just another painfully embarrassing situation to endure. And this is true of Coady's female characters as well. At the beginning of *Strange Heaven*, Bridget's constipation out-weighs her recent delivery of an unwanted child; while in one of *Hellgoing*'s stories, a writer-in-residence not only clogs her toilet on the first day but has to be reminded by the program director of her need to shower. Shame and humiliation are recurring traits, Coady's characters echoing each other throughout the stories. *Mean Boy*'s cousin Janet, for instance, claims a false pregnancy to justify her weight gain with her family, while Bridget never discusses the real child she gave up for adoption. The two characters' names even end with the same sylla-ble—*et*—rendering the feminine, it seems, in the diminutive. Physical attributes, and sometimes names, thus point to moral dilemmas, embodying both self-embarrassment and the resistance to conform to standards of appearance or behaviour.

The Satirist

Humiliation is this novelist's preferred setting because it forces the characters to mutate, and, in a way, to do so in the open. Her stories are not tales of self-reinvention or extraordinary maturation, even though the process they portray often leads to a form of self-acceptance. They are tales of moulting, sloughing, almost physiological accounts of what goes on in one's mind during the process of taking one's measure. Yet the older characters surrounding the protagonists make it all too clear that there is no improving with age. The good old grandma is just plain mean, as ready to punch you in the face as cold hard reality; the idolized professor no more mature, nor wiser, than his first-year stu-dent. Though the reverse can also be true, the family member feared as judgmental revealing himself as simply kind: "Bridget had been bothered about what Albert might say, but surprisingly, he doted" (*Strange Heaven* 16). Still, like the small town, family is often the place where ordinary violence, or even aggressive or mute ignorance, is first encountered. Coady shows that angst, struggle, and transition are not stages between achieved states of living, but *are* states of living. No virtue is associated with them, no merit or bonus—except, some-times, the benefit of clarity, of letting go of one's fake idols. Success and emancipation, then, are no longer to be a star football player, but to be able to leave the nondescript small place where one has grown up, or sometimes even to return to care for an ailing father (again as in *The Antagonist*). Or to be published. Or to be married, in a relationship, happy, not drinking, not violent, not obsessive, not caught up in a cult. Or, for a time, to be accepted by a group of acquaintances who could even pass for friends (as in *Mean Boy* and *Strange Heaven*).

This satirical reduction of our tendency to self-aggrandize—the splendid ridicule of the great poet-striving-for-tenure in *Mean Boy* comes to mind—reveals that this loose world of human failures, of friendships and betrayals, is guided by little more than the survival of the fittest, a harsh realization to which most characters come. But this reality is acutely funny, containing an endless potential for humour and a dark kind of self-derision. If it is a tragedy, it is a pedestrian one, terrible but inglorious, desperate yet modest: mocking the very tragedy of human existence with all of its supposed causality and significance.

In this respect, the deep undercurrent of faith in relation to religion is another element of the satire at work in Coady's writing, although an ambiguous one. It serves both as a cultural background to the isolated communities depicted, and as a philosophical backdrop for the questioning of free will *versus* destiny and fate. It is tempting to interpret the role of religion as a sarcastic one, pointing to the strange illusions and beliefs through which one tries to tighten the loose fabric of life. But there is also tenderness in how some of the true believers are portrayed, with their awkward, bigger-than-life generosity (Beth in *The Antagonist*) that makes the reader pause and wonder about the writer's intention or the aim of the stories. "It seemed as if things were happening without much reason or point" (7), *Strange Heaven* begins; while *Hellgoing* as a title might name the general direction towards which Coady's characters are headed, either in the Christian sense or in the colloquial sense of *to hell with it all!*

Overall, Coady's representation of religion poses the question of a higher meaning. Is physical strength designed to serve a purpose, or is it only random? Is there a greater force at the wheel, or is one entirely left to one's own devices? Do people relate to one another out of pure chance? Or is there a sense of fate associated with their encounter, or with the place they were born, or with the parents they were born from, or with the sex they were born in? Do they, and can they, determine their own destiny, just as Bridget escapes her pregnancy? How much of these experiences is happenstance, and how much determines who we are? It is this very indeterminacy that ties the latest novel, *The Antagonist*, with the first, *Strange Heaven*.

On Virility

The wit and satirical humour of Lynn Coady's writing is also expressed through situations and language. Such situations are created by an imbalance of power that reveals a character's insecurities and vulnerabilities: relationships between father and son, teacher and student, or established and aspiring poet. These give rise to the manoeuvering of weight (again, sometimes literally) over another human being, and move between the pathetic and the poignant. The language is often coarse and uncensored, complete with crude descriptions of being sick from too much drinking, pointing again to physical metamorphosis as literal embodiments of internal turmoil. Moreover, this crudity is what instantly gives the characters their *voice*—vulgar and funny, compelling and realistic—and insight into the flaws, vanities, and prejudices in themselves or in others. The coarseness conveyed both by the (often politically incorrect) language and by the matter of brute force informs the unfinished quality shared by many of the characters, a quality that gives them agency despite their limited circumstances, and lends the novels and stories, and especially their endings, again their fair amount of ambiguity.

There is a feminist streak in Coady's novels. At first glance, it may seem to reside in the unabashed liberty she takes with the English language through her use of the vernacular and her unconstrained depictions of the familiar. But her concern is mostly with male gender roles and stereotypes. Perfectly at ease with representing male insecurities and vulnerabilities, she is also deft in her depiction of the inherent violence of boyhood: cliques fraught with fear and competition, from local gangs to university frat boys, from small-time thugs to promising students, the two sometimes mingling. These crowds seem to portray a subspecies struggling for its own survival, haunted by a mirroring of anxieties passed from overbearing fathers to bullied sons, until a character cannot know whether he himself or his doppelgän-ger is the *Mean Boy* or *The Antagonist*. The contradictions and dilemmas associated with the need to "become a man" often provide the engine for drama, as well as the deployment of a spectrum of masculinities, from protective to abusive and, more rarely, equitable. It is no surprise to open *Saints of Big Harbour* to find as its epigraph a varying definition of "guy" and "guys," ranging from the example of "a nice guy" to illus-trate the singular; to the transitive verb meaning "to ridicule" as well as "to guide"; and then the informal designation of "Persons of either sex." If Coady has chosen, after her first novel was too closely identi-fied with memoir, to mainly inhabit male characters (Endicott 210), she nonetheless still navigates the ever-shifting ethos of a search-ing self through both masculine and feminine perspectives (as in the collection *Hellgoing*). While her non-heroic creatures generally fail at whatever script they were handed, it is precisely through their revealed vulnerabilities that we come to care so much for them. And there is virility, or courage, in *manning up* to this task. Lynn Coady's characters are *our* doppelgängers: they open up so we can look inside, at the fabric of our flawed humanity.

Works Cited

Coady, Lynn. *The Antagonist*. Toronto: House of Anansi Press, 2011. Print.

——. *Hellgoing*. Toronto: House of Anansi Press, 2013. Print.

——. *Mean Boy*. 2006. Toronto: Anchor Canada, 2007. Print.

——. *Saints of Big Harbour*. Toronto: Doubleday Canada, 2002. Print.

——. *Strange Heaven*. 1998. Reader's Guide Edition. With an afterword by Marina Endicott. Fredericton, NB: Goose Lane Editions, 2010. Print.

Endicott, Marina. "An Interview with Lynn Coady." *Strange Heaven*. Reader's Guide Edition. With an afterword by Marina Endicott. Fredericton, NB: Goose Lane Editions, 2010. 206–10. Print.

The Antagonist (excerpt)

SURPRISE! RANK HERE.

Adam, this has begun—there's no way around it. That's what I've been realizing this past week. I gave up writing to you and I felt this incredible relief—no doubt you did too. In fact that was the only thing that tainted my relief—knowing you were probably relieved as well. But fuck it, it was over! It had been started, but now it was stopped, and so was over. Cooler heads prevailed and all that. I'd just go back to doing what I've been doing all along—working and coaching and going to the gym—and you would go back to whatever it is you do—vampiring the good and the real out of people's lives—and we'd forget about each other as we'd already done and should've kept right on doing.

So let's take another run at this, shall we? I've been reading over what I sent you so far trying to figure out why in God's name I can't just settle into a nice, neat, chronological version of the story of my life. I keep going off on these pointless tangents. It seemed like such a simple idea at first—all I had to do was sit down and write it out. But it's actually a lot harder than you would think.

Now that I've read everything over, however, the problem has become clear. It appears I'd rather talk about pretty much anything other than working for Gord at the Icy Dream. But if I don't the rest of the story can't happen. Which is precisely the hurdle, come to think of it.

The interesting thing about this whole process is that I find myself realizing what I think about everything at the exact moment I'm typing it out. Then I sit back and read it over and go: *Huh.*

Is that how it works for you? This never really occurred to me before. I have to admit I kind of imagined you sitting around rubbing your hands together and cackling to yourself as you plotted out your miserable theft, not just typing away and suddenly looking down and going, Oh hey, check that out. I just completely screwed over a guy I used to be buddies with.

And I've also just realized that even though my outrage resulting from the above has led me to launch myself at you across the ether hollering *Hey nice story you thieving bastard but guess what, I have the real story right here—so get comfortable, chump!* That is, even though I was completely gung-ho when I initiated this little back and forth between us, there is a big part of me that keeps trying to bow out.

But I am going to do this, Adam. Neither of us is getting out of it. Every time I think fuck this and fuck you—and I think it with approximately every other sentence—I imagine your relief at never having to open another email from me and it propels me right back here in front of my ancient computer, constantly hitting the wrong keys and having to go back and start again in all my enthusiastic umbrage.

| Gord used to go over the counter. That was the crux of the matter. I had two jobs at Icy Dream—well, three, if you counted working the till and manoeuvring the soft-serve into two perfect undulating bulges balanced in the cone—three bulges if the customer ordered a large. That was something I eventually got very good at, executing perfectly undulating soft-serve—I felt like a sculptor at times. So I did that, I even took a bit of pride in it, but I was mostly at Icy Dream, according to Gord, to "bust punks' skulls." So I busted punks' skulls, but I also

had a third job, a private job that I had not been assigned but ended up inevitably assigning to myself.

And that was to keep Gord from going over the counter.

The problem, which my father could not have foreseen when the Celestial Fast-Food Overseer descended from the heavens and demanded he choose between ID and JJ's, was the existence of punks. Punks abounded in our town, as they do all towns, big and small, and were the bane of Gord's existence as a small-business owner.

Everywhere kids went in our town they promptly got thrown out of, was the thing. Nobody wanted teenagers anywhere out in public. I knew because I was one. I was the worst kind of teenager—superficially speaking, that is—the kind that grownups like the look of least. Big and thuggy. I could take them. I could take anyone, obviously. And if you put me with another two or three guys, no matter what the size of the others might be, we were terrifying. We were punks.

I remember getting thrown out of the mall once—for doing precisely nothing. We'd been sitting on one of the benches outside the Pizza Hut waiting for it to be time to go to a dance when a cop sauntered up carrying a grease-pocked bag of garlic fingers and told us to get lost. Our very existence was offensive to the other mall patrons, he explained. They couldn't abide the sight of us, a clutch of jean-jacketed menace huddled on the bench.

The cop didn't call our parents or curse us out and it was, as far as this kind of thing went, a pretty innocuous incident, which is why I didn't think it was something I should keep from Gord. But it turned out it was. When I mentioned it the next day at dinner he took a fit. I didn't raise you to be a goddamn punk, he screamed, handing me a bowl of mashed turnips. So why are you going around hanging out in the mall like a goddamn punk?

I wasn't doing it like a goddamn punk, I protested. We were just sitting here.

Sitting there like a goddamn punk! Give me the salt! Like you got nothing better to do!

I *don't* have anything better to do.

Then get your ass home if you don't have anything better to do! Help your mother! Do your homework! Straighten up your goddamn room! Where the fuck is the butter?

And so forth. There was no arguing with Gord on the punk front, not since he opened Icy Dream. Punks streamed in at all hours, hot and cold running punks, and Gord discovered his group nemesis. They scared off the kind of customers Gord wanted—moms with kids, for example, not to mention the considerable number of people who shuffled in solo just to buy a single cone or hot fudge sundae, some small confection to brighten up their lonely, ho-hum lives. These customers were depressing, yes, but at least they didn't make trouble. There is not much sadder than a fat guy in his fifties sitting alone in the back of an Icy Dream plastic-spooning soft-serve into his mouth, but there is one thing sadder, and that's watching the same guy flinch every time the jolly group of teenage dicks in the next booth erupt into gales of comradely yet somehow malicious laughter.

The punks would invariably order small orange pops and skulk in the corner booths spinning coins and shooting the shit under their breath until the gales of brain-dead testosterone-stupid laughter erupted, a sound that was like the pig-squeal of microphone feedback to my father's ears. For a while he tried the "Eat something or get out" tactic, at which point the punks would invariably pool their change and place a single order of small fries to see them through the next hour of customer alienation.

Get the hell over there, Gord would hiss at me then, and tell those punks to pound salt. Or else you'll bust their skulls, tell them.

They have drinks, I'd say.

They don't have drinks! They got a cup full of gob after chewing on their goddamn straws the last hour. Put your hat back on.

Usually when I had to confront the punks I would remove my paper hat because it made me feel like a tit.

I look like a tit in the hat, Gord. They won't take me seriously.

You don't look like a tit in the hat! It's your uniform. A uniform gives a man an air of authority.

An Icy Dream uniform does *not* give a man an air of authority.

You take pride in that uniform. You have nothing to be ashamed of. That uniform puts food on the—

Oh Jesus, I'm going. I'm going, Gord.

Stop calling me that! If you're too cool to say Dad you can damn well call me Mr. Rankin.

Calling him Gord was still a new habit at that point. I'd acquired it not long after I turned fifteen. It hadn't been intentional, the first time I'd done it—I can't even remember what the circumstance was—but once it was out and in the air between us I could tell I had kind of broken Gord's heart. After that I couldn't seem to stop.

Hi guys, I would greet the punks.

And what would happen next depended entirely on the punks in question. Sometimes the punks were my friends. They would smile up at me with their greasy, fry-fed faces, make an ungenerous remark or two about my hat and I would respond with a cheerful threat to shove my hat up their asses. After some back and forth along these lines I would tell them they should come back between around five and seven next time because that's when Gord went home for supper and then we could all hang out and I would give them free Cokes if they were nice to me.

Meanwhile, I'd say by way of wrapping things up, my dad requests you remove your dirty punk asses from his family establishment.

But Rank, Scott was thinking he might like a fudgy bar. He hasn't quite decided yet.

We don't want your business, boys. You bring the tone down. Bad optics, scuzz like you chowing down on our fudgies.

Why don't you chow down on one of *my* fudgies sometime, Rank?

Ha ha ha. Oh my god. Nice one. Get out.

And the guys would snort and smirk just so not to lose face entirely, then shuffle their way out the door taking care to look extra dangerous and sullen for the benefit of Gord, scowling away by the fryer.

Those were the good days.

On the bad days, guys like Mick Croft showed up.

Mick Croft was one of the town punks who actually *was* a punk—not just a gangly, belligerent, functionally retarded teenage boy like the rest of us. He dealt drugs—of course—and brandished knives—of course—and had been expelled for kicking the gym teacher, a man with the unfortunate name of Mr. Fancy, in the ass when Fancy was bending over to gather the volleyballs into a canvas sack. Fancy had just called Croft a loser in front of the whole class. Take a good look, guys, he'd said, at what not to be if you want to achieve anything in this life other than a welfare cheque. And then Fancy made the unbelievable move of turning around to get the volleyballs and showing Croft his sinewy glutes. It was like, Croft is rumoured to have protested, the man was offering it up.

That was the effect Croft had on adults—he enraged them, moved them to say the kind of things you should never say to a sixteen-year-old kid, no matter how much he pisses you off. Men in particular he provoked to tantrums. Croft had flunked enough grades to be in a couple of classes with me and I remember the entire room sucking in breath when a red-faced Geography teacher took hold of either side of Croft's desk—with him in it—and yanked it with an effortlessness born of pure animal rage to the front of the classroom. When everyone was going around asking what had prompted Fancy to denounce Croft like that in the gym it turned out to be because Croft had forgotten his shorts at home. Which sounds like nothing, but we all understood how little the shorts would have had to do with it. What it had to do with was Croft's attitude. Croft had a smirk that made you want to take hold of either side of his mouth and pull his face apart. It wasn't a smirk like that of other punks. It was a smart smirk, and was usually accompanied by a smart remark. And when I say smart, I mean *smart*. Croft wasn't your typical idiot punk like say his compadre Collie Chaisson who did time in the Youth Centre for putting his fist through a convenience store window and leaving a multitude of perfect, dried-blood fingerprints polka-dotting the cash register.

So it was no surprise that Croft would be the first to send my father lunging over the counter at Icy Dream, hands clenched to throttle and punch—simultaneously if at all possible. I will never forget that first time, grabbing Gord around the waist like a child and hoisting him backward as every muscle in his tiny body strained in the opposite direction. He actually had a boot on the counter at one point, but instead of using the leverage to launch himself at Croft, he was thwarted by me hauling him back at just the right moment and using the momentum against him. Croft was wide-eyed, having shot a good three feet back from the counter, skeezy smile quickly affixed to mask his shock. In his mind he was already sitting in some sweaty basement telling the story to Chaisson and his other dirtbag friends. Gordon Rankin man! Little fucker comes at me right over the fuckin counter man! Lost it. You goddamn punk! You little asshole! Like he can't even talk he's so pissed. Like in-co-*her*-ent with rage. So I'm ready to go right? Grown man coming straight at me, fuckit, he's the one who'll be charged, not me. I'm just a widdle kid. Lucky for him the gland-case comes to the rescue.

No one had ever called me a gland-case before I met Croft. I remember being a little shocked by it—the audacity. It wasn't the kind of town where guys got mocked for being big. You got mocked for wearing colourful shirts, or using words with more than two syllables, but not for being big. Big was considered an achievement. Total strangers all but stopped me on the street and congratulated me on it. Croft was the first person to make me feel like a freak.

I remember walking by him at a dance. Croft started bouncing up and down and making earthquake noises. I glanced around and grinned to show I got the joke, but also to let him know I had heard the joke and to determine if it was the kind of joke that required me to walk over there and set a few things straight. Croft grinned back at me. Huge and chimp-like. At which point I stopped smiling, allowed myself to slow down a little, upon which Croft held his hands up in the air, all innocence and goodwill.

I kept walking. *Fucking gland-case,* I eventually heard, enunciated loudly and with care from somewhere behind me. When I turned around, Croft and his cronies had dissolved into the crowd.

| Here's a snippet of how the conversation went between Croft and Gord moments before my father's attempt to take flight.

GORD: What can I get you today, son?

CROFT: Coke.

GORD: I beg your pardon, now, I didn't quite catch that.

CROFT: Coke.

GORD: You'd like a Coke, would you?

I should explain that Gord is already doing a slow burn at this point. I can all but hear the rant bubbling away in the foreground of his brain: *goddamn little Christer no respect doesn't even know how to ask for something it's the parents off doing god knows what don't even instill common courtesy let alone basic please and thank you think the world owes them every goddamn thing they get.* So it's only at this point that Croft, who has been paying no attention whatsoever up until now, actually turns his nasty focus on my father. So I see this. I am standing at the grill supposedly waiting for it to be time to turn the patties over but at this point I have pretty much forgotten about the patties because I witness the way Croft's bright little eyes are taking full measure of Gord and the tendrils of smoke slowly wafting from my father's ears.

No, I think. Not the smirk.

Croft allows the smirk to just kind of ooze across his face like syrup on pancakes.

CROFT (enunciating loudly, precisely the way he did when he called me a gland-case at the dance): Yeah, bud. I said a Coke. *Coca. Cola.* I wanna teach the world to sing.

(Chortles from the skeezer crew lined up behind him.)

GORD (with a hideous patience that tells me he is reveling in the accumulation of adrenalin that's taking place as his ire is stirred. Now the two of them are practically dancing together): It's not that I can't hear you, son. I may have a few years on you, but I don't have any trouble with my hearing.

(Oh Christ, I think, he's called him "son" again.)

CROFT: Sorry, bud. Guess it must be the Alzheimer's setting in or something.

(More skeezer tittering. Even though it isn't quite time, I rapidly flip all the patties on my grill to get this particular obligation out of the way.)

GORD: My problem, *son*, is with you. And the fact that you little assholes keep coming in here...

CROFT: (flipping his hands into the air at the word "assholes"): I just want a Coke! I'm just thirsty!

GORD: ...and you sit in the back corner both scaring people away and reeking of maryjane...

CROFT: I don't even know Mary Jane! I never touched her!

(skeezers holding their sides at this point)

GORD: ...and then you have the goddamn nerve to come up here and grunt at me in my own restaurant. "Coke" (Neanderthal grunt-speak here). "Coke, *bud*. Gimme Coke."

CROFT: Look, *bud*...

That's what did it. The slavering insolence of that third and final "bud." I dropped my flipper and hurled myself forward, reaching Gord just before his extended hands could secure themselves around Croft's neck.

There was a lot of yelling. The word "punks" occasionally leapt like a salmon from an otherwise undifferentiated stream of obscenities where my father was concerned, whereas on Croft's side of the counter, as he and his crew sauntered (but sauntered somewhat hurriedly, I'd like to point out) toward the door, I heard—along with their own laughing, obscene stream—the words "Crazy" and "...should call the fuckin cops!"

Once Croft et al. had taken off, I yelled—still clinging to Gord—something around the restaurant about complimentary single cones for everybody, but everybody was too busy gathering up their bug-eyed children and herding them toward the exists to notice. The only people left to take advantage of the offer were a few workers from SeaFare grabbing burgers after their shift, and they seemed to regard the incident as a kind of floor show. They laughed and applauded and generally made me regret the free ice cream I ended up doling out to them.

"Nice reflexes there, Rankin."

"You shoulda let him go off on that little tool."

"Why you giving my food away to those assholes?" Gord wanted to know once I had rejoined him behind the counter. He had yelled at me for burning my patties but otherwise seemed cheerful and refreshing after his lunge at Croft, like he'd just woken up from a nap.

"Because you attacked one of the customers," I explained. "Those assholes are only ones who didn't run screaming out the door."

"'Customer' my ass, goddamn little punk! *Sorry, bud. Coke, bud.* They oughta give me a medal."

So about twenty-five minutes later, a pair of Mounties came strolling through the door.

"Here they come," I said. "They got your medal, Gord."

MICHAEL CRUMMEY is among the Rock's most powerful voices, with a writing infused by humour, charm, magic realism, and lyrical longing. He was born in 1965 in Buchans, Newfoundland, and moved in the late 1970s to the mining town of Wabush, near the Labrador–Québec border. Crummey later attended Memorial University in Newfoundland, where he was awarded first place in the Gregory J. Power Poetry Competition in 1986. His first poem was published in the literary journal *TickleAce*, a publication that focused mainly on Newfoundland and Labrador writing. After earning a bachelor of arts with a major in English in 1987, Crummey attended Queen's University in Kingston, Ontario, where he completed a master of arts in 1988, then left the doctoral program to pursue a career in writing. In 1994, he won the inaugural Bronwen Wallace Award for Poetry for emerging writers under the age of thirty-five. That same year he was also runner-up in the *PRISM International* Short Fiction Contest. His first collection of poetry, *Arguments with Gravity* (Quarry Press, 1996), won the Writers' Alliance of Newfoundland and Labrador Literary Award for Poetry. Crummey's second collection, *Hard Light* (Brick Books, 1998), reimagines his family history and considers lost ways of life in Newfoundland and Labrador and was nominated for the 1999 Milton Acorn People's Poetry Award. That same year, Crummey published *Flesh*

and Blood (Beach Holme Publishing, 1998; Anchor Canada, 2003), the collection from which a story was selected for the *Journey Prize Anthology 10* (McClelland & Stewart, 1998). Crummey's first novel, *River Thieves* (Doubleday, 2001), met critical acclaim. It won the Thomas Head Raddall Award, the Winterset Award for Excellence in Newfoundland Writing, and the Atlantic Independent Booksellers' Choice Award. It was also short-listed for the Giller Prize, the Commonwealth Writers' Prize, the *Books in Canada* First Novel Award, and was longlisted for the International IMPAC Dublin Literary Award. A chapbook of poetry, *Roadside Emergency Assistance* (Trout Lily Press, 2001), was published that same year. His sec-ond novel, *The Wreckage* (Doubleday Canada, 2005), was longlisted for the 2007 IMPAC Award. *Galore* (Random House of Canada, 2009), Crummey's sprawling, mythic family saga of Newfoundland, was awarded the 2010 Commonwealth Writers' Prize for Best Book (Canada & Caribbean), the 2010 Canadian Authors Association Literary Award, and was shortlisted for the 2010 Atlantic Independent Booksellers' Choice and the 2011 IMPAC Award. He published his most recent collection of poetry, *Under the Keel*, with House of Anansi Press in 2013. His fourth novel, *Sweetland* (Doubleday, 2014), was shortlisted for the Governor General's Award for Fiction. In 2004, Crummey collaborated with photographer Greg Locke on *Newfoundland: Journey into a Lost Nation* (McClelland & Stewart, 2004), and in 2014 with the National Film Board of Canada to research and write the short film *54 Hours*, co-directed by Paton Francis and Bruce Alcock, about the 1914 Newfoundland Sealing Disaster. His writing has appeared in a number of publications, including *The Fiddlehead, TickleAce, The Malahat Review, PRISM International, Poetry Canada, Grain, Descant, The New Quarterly*, and *The Walrus*. Crummey's work has also been anthologized in *Victory Meat: New Fiction from Atlantic Canada* (Anchor Canada, 2003) and *Running the Whale's Back: Stories of Faith and Doubt from Atlantic Canada* (Goose Lane Editions, 2013), among several other collections. In 2007, Crummey was honoured with the Writers' Trust of Canada Timothy Findley Award, which recognized his entire body of work. He now lives and writes in St. John's, Newfoundland. Michael Crummey visited the Canadian Literature Centre for his Brown Bag Lunch reading on November 19, 2014.

3

MICHAEL CRUMMEY
The Presence of the Past

JENNIFER BOWERING DELISLE

"UNLIKE ANYWHERE ELSE I've ever been in Canada," Michael
Crummey says of his home province of Newfoundland, "the past is
who we are." It is to this profound presence of the past that Crummey
attributes his interest in historical fiction and poetry ("Latest Novel").
The "visceral" awareness that "we have been made by the people who
came before us" permeates Crummey's work, not only in setting but in
recurring themes of loss and home. This is not to suggest, as the prov-
ince's own tourism ads sometimes have, that Newfoundland is an
anachronism—that it is somehow stuck in the past, immune to change
and the influence of the rest of the world. Crummey's work is invested
in history not only as a record of what has been, but also as a narrative
of change. Much of his writing grapples with cultural and ethical ques-
tions about how the past is remembered and preserved, and how we
come to terms with it as a part of who we are.

Sweetland (2014) is Crummey's first truly contemporary novel. Yet it
clearly demonstrates the profound influence of the past on its charac-
ters and communities. Sweetland is both the name of the protagonist
and the name of the fictional island off Newfoundland's coast on
which the novel is set. It is not uncommon for small communities
to be named after the families that built them, but in this novel the

congruence has deeper meaning. Place, here, and two hundred years of ancestry in that place, are vital to personal identity.

The failure of cod stocks over the twentieth century, which culminated in a moratorium on the fishery in 1992, has caused a steady decline in the populations of Newfoundland's outports, its small fishing communities. Less than fifty people remain in Chance Cove, the main village on the island of Sweetland. All of Chance Cove has chosen to take advantage of a government resettlement program and abandon their isolated home—all but Sweetland the man. As the single holdout, he stands in the way of his neighbours receiving a $100,000 payout. Increasingly isolated from his community, Sweetland becomes an island to match his namesake. In the passage excerpted here, Sweetland has finally announced that he will join the program, though his intention is to fake his death in order to stay behind in his home.

This resettlement program is a reprise of infamous programs in the decades following confederation with Canada in 1949, designed to relocate people to larger communities where services could be provided more cheaply. By the mid-1970s, more than a quarter of Newfoundland's communities had been abandoned. Resettlement also figures in Crummey's 2005 novel *The Wreckage*, in which the "wreckage" of the buildings in an abandoned community (306) is emblematic of the wreckage of personal lives and relationships in the aftermath of the Second World War. In *Sweetland*, the new version of resettlement is similarly destructive. In the passage reproduced in this anthology, Sweetland visits the site of Tilt Cove, which was resettled when he was a boy. As Sweetland wanders the remains of the community, we glimpse the inevitable fate of his home: "depressions to show where the houses and root cellars had been, the overgrown outline of shale foundations. Not a board or shard of glass or shingle otherwise, all of it scavenged or rotted or blown to hell and gone." When Sweetland tells the bureaucrat trying to convince him to move that "people been fishing here two hundred years or more. I expect my crowd was the first ones on the island" (9), he gestures towards the magnitude of this loss.

In his 2009 novel *Galore*, Crummey creates another fictional community to narrate these two centuries of outport life, including unique

cultural practices, the exploitative fishing industry, the establish-
ment of the Fishermen's Protective Union, and the devastating loss of
young men in the First World War. This historical world is coloured
by magic realism. The novel begins with the discovery of a naked man
alive in the belly of a beached whale. He is given the name Judah and
taken in by the Devine family, despite the reek of fish that he will carry
the rest of his life. As the generations continue, patterns repeat. But
the characters we have followed become for their descendants hazy
and mysterious tales from the past—legends as fantastical as Judah's
survival. We witness not only two hundred years of history but the
making of folklore. Crummey explains,

> I wanted *Galore* to mirror this weird little circle where Newfoundlanders
> are the people that created these stories that have been passed
> down, but now those stories are creating Newfoundlanders. My
> sense of who I am as a Newfoundlander and what it means to be a
> Newfoundlander comes from hearing those stories. ("Company")

Crummey also gathers and reimagines those stories of life in early
twentieth-century Newfoundland in his collection of short fiction,
Flesh and Blood (1998), in a section of his poetry collection *Under the Keel*
(2013), and in his collection of verse and prose poetry *Hard Light* (1998).
But in the latter work, stories of Newfoundland's past also generate
a sense of distance and loss. Anxiety about what has been forgot-
ten recurs, a theme established in the first poem, "Rust." Here a boy
watches his father's hands:

> They have a history the boy knows nothing of, another life they have
> left behind. Twine knitted to mend the traps, the bodies of codfish
> opened with a blade, the red tangle of life pulled from their bellies.
> Motion and rhythms repeated to the point of thoughtlessness, map
> of a gone world etched into the unconscious life of his hands by
> daily necessities, the habits of generations. (9)

The nostalgia in these poems is not a desire to return to the difficult labour of catching and drying fish, but a desire for traditional knowledge that promises a kind of belonging. In his essay "Journey into a Lost Nation" (2004), Crummey reflects on the depth of loss that the fishery collapse has meant; beyond the devastating economic repercussions, "something at the very centre of our sense of ourselves has been permanently altered" (35).

The demise of the fishery has led not only to the resettlement of rural communities but to the large-scale out-migration of Newfoundlanders to other parts of Canada in search of work. In our passage from *Sweetland*, Sweetland recalls the "diaspora of economic refugees" who returned to visit, flaunting their new wealth and disingenuously claiming "how much they missed Newfoundland." He also recalls the moment he decided to join them, to head to "fucken old Toronto" for the enticing wage of $1.50 an hour. On a personal level, an accident that befalls Sweetland while away changes the course of his life. But his time in Ontario's construction sites and steel mills is also reflective of a continuous stream of out-migration that has plagued Newfoundland for well over a century (see Delisle, *The Newfoundland Diaspora*). And it is an earlier manifestation of the hard life that sees the Priddles, two young brothers from Chance Cove, working "a seesaw contract in Fort McMurray, three or four weeks on the job, two weeks off to fly home and drink and smoke and snort all the money they'd made" (56). As Chance Cove is abandoned, Sweetland's neighbours move not just to St. John's but to other provinces, to the places where their children have already relocated. If personal identity is tied to twelve generations of lineage in a place, then leaving that place is much more than a change to the colour of your driver's licence. It is, for many, a profound loss. Having lived away from Newfoundland himself for more than a decade, Crummey reflects, "it still isn't unusual, when asking Newfoundlanders where they're from, to hear them say they 'belong to Newfoundland.' It's a telling linguistic tic. Our connection to the place is a tie that seems more filial than simple citizenship" (*Newfoundland* 18).

But this claim to a belonging rooted in centuries of history is also problematic for a settler-invader society. In his first novel, *River Thieves* (2001), Crummey self-consciously looks back at a settler expedition that ends in the murder of two Beothuk men and the kidnapping of Mary March (Demasuit), a young Beothuk mother. The "extinction" of the Beothuk people has been the subject of much Newfoundland literature, often, as Mary Dalton argues, treating "the Indian as emblem: the Noble Savage, the spirit of Nature, the past, the timeless, death, the source of wound for the European colonizers" (144). Ironically, the colonizers' complicity in the Beothuk's demise is often refigured as their descendants' primordial loss. Terry Goldie argues that the annihilation of the Beothuk enables a unique process of "indigenization": "The argument might be interpreted as 'We had natives. We killed them off. Now we are natives'" (157). Crummey's novel attempts to complicate this move, refusing to provide his settler characters with a retroactive belonging to the land, while also eschewing a simplistic colonial guilt.

One of Crummey's main strategies in complicating the past is to highlight the flaws in the historical record. Late in the novel, the protagonist reflects, "two hundred years from now, he knew, some stranger could raise his bones from the earth and put whatever words they liked in his mouth" (347). Crummey himself is this stranger, writing two hundred years later, and this metafictional moment invites readers to question how the past is recorded and recreated. *River Thieves* demonstrates that this dark colonial past has a profound influence on Newfoundland identity, not just in a nostalgic, romanticized rendering of the Beothuk as lost ancestors, but in an ongoing sense of unsettlement. If the past is "who Newfoundlanders are," then this identity is one that can be self-consciously constructed, contradictory, and changing.

Alone in Chance Cove with little to do, Sweetland begins reading a book that one of his neighbours was sent by her daughter:

Half an hour later he was ready to throw the bloody thing in the stove....He looked at the cover each time he quit reading, flipped it to inspect the back. A quote from a Toronto paper about "authentic Newfoundland." Whoever wrote the book didn't know his arse from a dory, Sweetland figured, and had never caught or cleaned a fish in his life. (206)

In another instance of metafiction, Crummey prompts us to question how the book that we are reading constructs "authentic Newfoundland"; in an interview Crummey admits that "in an earlier version of *Sweetland*, the book was *Galore*. That's me he's talking to" ("Company"). In rendering the authenticity of what we are reading suspect, Crummey leads us to ask, is there even such a thing as "authentic Newfoundland?" If there is, and it is constituted by dories and catching and cleaning fish, what is the future of Newfoundland in the face of resettlement, out-migration, and the death of the fishery? And if there isn't, to what should Newfoundlanders look to define themselves?

In the same interview Crummey says that he "used to worry that the move toward urbanization and the loss of these communities was going to mean homogenization, and Newfoundland was going to be just like everything else." But he has stopped worrying about the change, in part because of his own children: "I've become aware of the fact that even though these kids are growing up in a world where they're raised on the Internet, and 200 American cable channels...when I look at them, what I see is Newfoundlanders. They are still of that place" ("Company"). To be of that place, for Crummey, is to acknowledge the influence of the past and to be self-reflective about that influence. It is to recognize that the present shapes our understanding of the past as much as the past has shaped the present. And it is to regard the past not as the source of some authentic essence at risk of being lost, but as part of an ongoing narrative of change.

Works Cited

Crummey, Michael. *Flesh and Blood*. 1998. Toronto: Anchor, 2003. Print.

———. *Galore*. Toronto: Anchor, 2009. Print.

———. *Hard Light*. London: Brick Books, 1998. Print.

——. "In the Company of the Dead: An Interview with Michael Crummey." Interview by Anna Fitzpatrick. *Hazlitt* 2 Sept. 2014. Web. 27 Feb 2015.

——. "Journey into a Lost Nation." *Newfoundland: Journey into a Lost Nation.* Ed. Michael Crummey and Greg Locke. Toronto: McClelland & Stewart, 2004. 7-39. Print.

——. "Michael Crummey on his Latest Novel, *Sweetland*." Interview by Karin Wells. CBC *Books* 3 Sept. 2014. Web. 27 Feb. 2015.

——. *River Thieves.* Toronto: Doubleday, 2001. Print.

——. *Sweetland.* Toronto: Doubleday, 2014. Print.

——. *Under the Keel.* Toronto: House of Anansi Press, 2013. Print.

——. *The Wreckage.* Toronto: Anchor, 2006. Print.

Dalton, Mary. "Shadow Indians: The Beothuk Motif in Newfoundland Literature." *Newfoundland Studies* 8.2 (1992): 135-46. Print.

Delisle, Jennifer. *The Newfoundland Diaspora: Mapping the Literature of Out-Migration.* Waterloo, ON: Wilfrid Laurier University Press, 2013.

Goldie, Terry. *Fear and Temptation.* Montréal and Kingston: McGill-Queen's University Press, 1989. Print.

Sweetland (excerpt)

THE WIND CAME UP through the day and the ocean chopped at them as soon as they cleared the bay on the return trip, the boat riding sluggish with a full load of wood. They swung into the lee of Little Sweetland as they passed, to get out of the worst of it a few minutes. The island humpbacked and barren and solitary. Two single-room cabins on the south side of Tilt Cove, satellite dishes screwed to the walls. Sweetland had never seen anyone use those cabins, though they'd been there for years.

"This is where they put the buffaloes," Jesse said.

Every time they passed Tilt Cove he wanted this fact confirmed and then insisted on hearing the story behind it, the narrative like a toll required to make the passage.

"This is the place."

"How many people was it lived here?" Jesse asked, which was a surprise to Sweetland. The boy had never shown the slightest interest in the detail before.

"There was almost a hundred lived in there when I was your age," Sweetland said.

"What happened to them?"

"They was all shifted out by the Smallwood government in the sixties."

"Where did they go?"

"Here and there," he said. "Placentia Bay. Burgeo Hermitage. St. John's."

"They're all dead now."

Sweetland nodded over that. He didn't know anymore where the boy's head was going to take things. "Most of them, I expect."

"You helped get them ashore," Jesse said.

"Who's that?"

"The buffaloes."

"It was as good as a concert," he said.

Just home from his first stint in Toronto and working as a deckhand on a schooner shipping dry goods and salt fish along the south coast. The *Ceciliene Marie*. They sailed across the strait to Cape Breton to pick up the bison, the animals harried into individual containers and a crane lifting them off the dock, setting them into an improvised pen in the hold. Two dozen altogether, most of them yearling females. Two bulls. Unlikely-looking things, a thousand pounds each and most of the weight in the massive head and shoulders, top-heavy on those stick legs. The opposite of icebergs, Sweetland thought, nine-tenths above the water. The animals were walleyed, drugged-up and stinking of shit and fear. Five had died in the railcar on the trip from Manitoba, and Sweetland thought it would be a miracle if any survived the ocean crossing.

It was the wildlife department wanting to add another large game animal to the few in the province landed them there. They planned to set the bison out on Little Sweetland to determine there was no disease risk to local animals, after which the herd was meant to be introduced to the larger island of Newfoundland. Though that step was never taken.

The *Ceciliene Marie* sailed past Sweetland to overnight in Miquelon. They got drunk there, the wildlife officers and Sweetland, anchored off the last crumb of New France that was still a French territory. It was the only time he'd ever visited the place. The wildlife officers were all Newfoundlanders but for the fellow in charge, an American from Nevada who requested the stop in Miquelon. He took every chance he could get, he said, to spend a night in France.

Wet and mauzy when they arrived at Tilt Cove the following morning. Dozens of people had sailed out from Fortune Bay and the Burin to watch the event, the harbour packed with boats and spectators on the roofs of the houses still standing in the cove.

There was nowhere for the freighter to dock and they anchored off in deeper water, the buffalo loaded into their individual crates to be ferried ashore on a raft built by the wildlife officers. They'd hired Duke Fewer to tow the raft back and forth with his longliner. Sweetland was on the crane for the first dozen transfers, lowering the boxes onto the flat beside the schooner. The bison sedated and more or less quiet as they were hauled onto dry land. Staggering into the open with a stunned air about them, shaking those big rig shoulders and prancing drunkenly up away from the water. The people on the roofs hooting and shouting in disbelief as the mythological creatures wandered about in a forlorn herd, travelling and turning in a huddle, pawing at the sedge moss, sniffing the salt air.

"They aren't really buffaloes," Jesse announced.

"Is that right?" Sweetland said.

"Bison aren't related to water buffaloes or African buffaloes."

"What is it they're related to, then?"

"Cows," Jesse said. "And goats."

It was some Google search the boy was quoting, a universe of facts at his fingertips. As if, Sweetland thought, he wasn't tiresome enough on his own. "Be that as it may," he said, "does Your Highness mind if, for the purposes of this story, I calls them buffalo?"

"I don't mind," Jesse said.

Sweetland took a turn on the raft after lunch and he stood with a wildlife officer as each crate was floated in, holding the top of the box to keep his place on the narrow flat. Ashore, he stood at the rear as the officer opened the door. If it needed encouragement to step into the open, Sweetland prodded the animal's backside with a stick through a custom-made hole.

They'll come right through the wall if they minds to kick, the officer warned him, so watch yourself.

The animals had all been sedated in the morning but they seemed to be crawling out of that fog as the afternoon wore on. The next-to-last cow was bawling before she was lifted off the schooner, rocking the crate in the air. They cinched the container to the flat, the buffalo's hooves making the walls shake as they spidered around the outside. The smell and motion of the water seemed to unhinge her altogether and she slammed against the box as they started toward the landing site. All the wooden joints coming loose as the animal panicked inside, the container coming apart before they'd travelled thirty yards toward shore. The wildlife officer pitched into the water as the buffalo pushed for the clear and he grabbed a corner of the raft to hold himself afloat. Sweetland made a wild, stupid lunge for the animal's tail.

"As if I could have picked her up like a rat," he said to Jesse.

There wasn't room enough on the raft for the creature to turn around. She tried to catch herself at the edge but bowled over, top-heavy as she was. A splintered wall of the crate was floating beside the raft and the buffalo fell onto it, the wooden sheet tipping beneath her weight. Sweetland standing over her as she thrashed, trying to right herself. She went down slowly at first, submerging like a boat taking on water. But once she was under she sank like a stone, as if she was on a line and being dragged down from below. That dark face staring up at Sweetland on the surface, eyes wide, bubbles streaming from the massive nostrils. He could see her descending through the clear water for a long, long time.

"Could you see her on the bottom?" Jesse asked.

"Too deep out there near the schooner," he said. "Lost sight of her after awhile."

The rest of the animals survived the trip, but for one of the bulls who died within two days of the landing. Calves were born every spring and the remnants of the herd hung on for almost thirty years, though the buffalo never managed to take hold on the island. Sweetland would watch for them on the headlands as he passed by Little Sweetland, those shaggy outlines adrift in the mist like something called up from the underworld.

"What happened to them all?" Jesse asked.

"No one really knows. They used to walk out on the cliffs to lick the salt off the rocks. There's a good many got killed that way. Could be poachers took some of them."

The boy considered that possibility a moment. "You ever tasted buffalo?"

"Now, Jesse," he said. "That would be telling, wouldn't it."

...

Sweetland was up early the next morning and down to the wharf while the stars were still bright. He hadn't slept and couldn't lie still any longer. He took his chainsaw and gas can, though he had no real interest in cutting wood. He just wanted out of the cove before the news made the rounds.

He drove to Burnt Head and around the Fever Rocks, riding slow as the day's light came up on the world, without a notion as to where he was going or why. He went into the lee of Little Sweetland and stared up at the bare hillsides as he passed Tilt Cove. Not a sign to say where the dozens of houses and flakes and outbuildings once stood. He came about, chugged into the abandoned harbour. There was a wooden wharf kept up by the mysterious owners of the two cabins on the hill, and he tied up there.

Sweetland sat on the dock with a cup of tea from the thermos, waiting for the sun to lift the cove out of shadow. Walked up onto the beach then, strolled aimlessly across the hillside. The community's remains might have been a thousand years old for all that was left of them. There were depressions to show where the houses and root cellars had been, the overgrown outline of shale foundations. Not a board or shard of glass or shingle otherwise, all of it scavenged or rotted or blown to hell and gone. He tried to imagine the buildings in their places, tried to unearth the names of the people who'd lived in them. Dominies and Barters and Keepings.

He glanced toward the harbour now and then, trying to tell by its location which outline had been the Dolimounts' house. It was still standing the last occasion he'd come ashore with Duke Fewer—1966 that was, the first Come Home Year sponsored by the Smallwood government, a campaign to encourage the diaspora of economic refugees to spend their summer vacation at home in Newfoundland. Sweetland had given up working on the schooner to stay closer to Chance Cove at the time, fishing on Duke's longliner, and they'd had a poor season at it. Dozens of people coming back to the cove from the mainland as the fishery floundered. They flaunted their store-bought, handed out suitcases full of trinkets to the youngsters, talked hourly wages and hockey games at Maple Leaf Gardens and how much they missed Newfoundland. Most of them hadn't shown their faces home in a decade and Sweetland couldn't wait for the fuckers to leave.

He and Duke did some hook and line in the early fall and trawled through October, with barely enough luck to warrant the money they were spending on gas. They decided to go across to the Burin to try for moose. A cold rain on the barrens and no sign of a living thing to shoot at for three days. Spent their time tramping through sodden gorse and tuckamore, slept nights in a leaky tent not half big enough to accommodate Duke's appendages. They ate potted meat sandwiches on white bread, drank instant coffee laced with rye. Hands and feet numb from the unrelenting chill and every item of clothes they'd packed soaked through.

I've had enough of this bullshit, Duke said. They were crouched under a square of canvas angled over a scraggly fire, their fourth morning out, waiting for the kettle to boil.

Sweetland had his hands stretched to the flame but couldn't feel any heat coming off it at all. Be a long winter, he said, without a bit of moose meat put aside.

The winter won't be half as long as the last three days have been, Duke said.

They had a two-hour tramp back to the bay where they'd moored the boat and they walked it in silence, one behind the other. They piled all their gear in the wheelhouse and huddled there in misery as Sweetland nosed into open ocean. And they travelled most of the way back to Sweetland without speaking a word.

I been thinking about going up to Toronto, Duke said when Little Sweetland was in sight. Next spring sometime.

You talk to Ange about it?

Duke was recently married, just long enough for his wife to have the one child and be two months toward having a second.

Not yet, no.

What do you think she'll think of it?

Probably she'll be happy to be clear of me awhile.

Yes, Sweetland said. I finds women likes nothing better than being left alone to look after two young ones.

Duke stared across at him.

I'm only saying.

Well shut up out of it, for chrissakes, Duke said. And a moment later he said, You should come with me.

Sweetland shook his head. I hates fucken old Toronto, he said.

Fucken old Toronto pays a buck fifty an hour. Never going to make that kind of money at the fish.

They were swinging out around the cliffs of Little Sweetland, a cloud of mist like a shroud over the east end of the island.

It's Effie keeping you home, is it? Duke said.

We idn't married, Sweetland said.

Duke watched him a second. Jesus, he said, I'm gut foundered.

Sweetland looked up to the headlands and, sure enough, there were a handful of figures standing in the fog, their massive shadows motionless on the cliff edge.

Look up there, he said.

Where?

On the headland there.

Can't see a thing.

Just watch, Sweetland said.

And a moment later the shadowy creatures turned and moved off into the grey.

Jesus, what a size they are.

You think they're fit to eat? Duke asked.

They looks to me like they'd be tougher than the hobs of hell, Sweetland said, even if you managed to get them on a plate.

Duke shrugged. I don't mind chewing, he said.

Sweetland eased off the throttle outside the entrance to Tilt Cove, turned into the calmer water.

It's a big frigging island, Duke.

We'll just go for a stroll, he said. See what we can see.

They walked up out of the cove, following the old path to the pond on the high ground above the harbour, their woollen socks squelching in their boots.

Be hard to get a clear shot in this weather, Sweetland said.

They're big as barns. Pilgrim could probably pick one off.

The trail went through a trough of scrub spruce, not a single tree the height of Duke, but the branches crowding the path held tufts of hair pulled from the bison hides as the animals walked past. An hour to reach the headlands and nothing to see there but buffalo pies, some still steaming in the cold air.

They can't be far, Duke whispered.

They could be halfway to Hibb's Hole for all you knows.

They skirted the cliffs to the east end of the island, walking until they risked not getting back to the boat before dark. They hadn't eaten since morning and Sweetland could hear Duke's stomach grumbling as they cut across the island, the rolling echo like a distant thunder-storm. They walked down into the cove, along the side of one of the few houses still standing, the door long gone, the windowpanes beaten out by weather. Gotta take a leak, Sweetland said, and he turned to the wall out of the wind, let loose against the shale foundation while Duke waited two paces ahead.

This was the Dolimounts' place, Duke said idly. He was facing away from Sweetland, watching the cove. Jim Dolimount? he said. Married to Eunice?

Sweetland staring into the gloom as he pissed, nearly dark inside. The kitchen empty of furniture, the wallpaper stained and peeling. The floor littered with what looked to Sweetland to be buffalo patties, the animals using the building as a shelter to get out of the weather. He leaned to look through into the living room and his water went dry.

They had nine youngsters, Duke was saying, before Eunice had the hysterectomy into St. John's.

Duke, Sweetland whispered. He was tucking himself in but never glanced away, afraid the creature would disappear if he did. He reached for the rifle where he'd leaned it against the house, nosed the barrel into the frame to let it rest on the sill. The animal shifted on its feet, the hooves against the wood floor drumming in the hollow space.

What in the Jesus was that? Duke asked just as Sweetland fired. The rifle shot echoed in the empty room like a cannon, knocking the last pane of glass from the window. Duke was shouting but Sweetland couldn't hear anything over the ringing in his ears.

They tried to haul the buffalo out of the house before they dressed it, but there was no way to get the dead animal through the doorway. Duke brought up a storm lamp from the boat and they butchered the buffalo where it lay, the stink mushrooming in the enclosed space. They carried the quarters down to the water, the thigh bones like a stick over their shoulders, the massive parcel of meat lying pelt side down against their backs. Duke wanted to leave the rest of the carcass where it was but Sweetland wouldn't have it.

Those wildlife officers is out here two or three times a season, he said. I don't want anyone coming around Sweetland looking for poachers.

They dragged the head and spine across the threshold and down to the shoreline, throwing it into a fathom of water. They gathered up the shin bones and the mess of the internal organs in the bloody cloak of the pelt and tossed that into the cove as well, but for the heart and liver that they wrapped in a square of cloth and tucked away in Duke's pack. Sluiced the blood and offal out the door of the house with buckets of water. They crouched in the landwash then to clean the blood off their hands and forearms in the bitter cold of the ocean.

Dark now the once, Duke said. Maybe we should overnight here.

Sweetland shook his head. Darker the better, he said, given what we're carting.

I hope it don't taste like bear meat.

Sweetland glanced across at the man beside him. When have you ever tasted bear?

I haven't, he said. Just don't think I'd like it.

Duke stood and dried his arms on the wet sweater under his jacket, the burnished wedding ring glinting in the day's last light.

Maybe I'll come with you, Sweetland said then. Up to the mainland.

Duke watched him a few seconds, still drying his arms. I thought you hated fucken old Toronto?

Buck fifty an hour, like you says.

Sweetland couldn't say what possessed him to make that deci-sion, any more than he could explain why he'd called the government man to take the package when he did. There was no saying how things might have turned out if he'd stayed at home instead of going to Toronto. But it all went sideways there on Little Sweetland, the buffalo's blood still under his nails, his hands numb with the ocean's cold.

A life was no goddamn thing in the end, he thought. Bits and pieces of make-believe cobbled together to look halfways human, like some stick-and-rag doll meant to scare crows out of the garden. No goddamn thing at all.

CATERINA EDWARDS is an author of fiction, nonfiction, and drama, and one of Canada's best-known Italian Canadian writers. She was born in 1948 in Earls Barton, England, to an English father and an Italian mother, and as a result learned English and Italian simultaneously. She moved to Alberta with her parents as a child and grew up in Calgary while spending summers with her mother's family in Italy. Edwards attended the University of Alberta in Edmonton, where she received a bachelor of arts, honours in English. She then received a master of arts degree from the University of Alberta where she studied with Sheila Watson and Rudy Wiebe. While teaching at Grant MacEwan College, Edwards published her first novel, *The Lion's Mouth* (NeWest Press, 1982; Guernica Editions, 1993), which went on to be translated into French by Christiane Di Matteo and Jocelyn Doray as *La gueule du lion* (Balzac Editions, 2000). Edwards followed this novel with a play, *Homeground* (Guernica Editions, 1990), which was also professionally produced in a slightly altered form, titled *Terra Straniera* (Foreign land) at the 1986 Edmonton Fringe Festival. *Homeground* was also a finalist for the Gwen Pharis Ringwood Award for Drama in 1990. She then published two novellas, *A Whiter Shade of Pale* and *Becoming Emma* (NeWest Press, 1992). *Island of the Nightingales* (Guernica Editions, 2000), a collection of short stories, won the Howard O'Hagan Short Fiction Award. In 2002, her essay "What Remains" was awarded the Jon Whyte Essay Prize. Edwards also wrote *The Great Antonio*, a docudrama, for CBC Radio's *Sunday Showcase* in 2006. Alongside Kay Stewart, Edwards co-edited *Eating Apples: Knowing Women's Lives* (NeWest Press, 1994) and *Wrestling with the Angel: Women Reclaiming Their Lives* (Red Deer Press, 2000). Next, Edwards published *Finding Rosa* (Greystone, 2008), a work of creative nonfiction that documents her mother's life as she begins to show signs of Alzheimer's. *Finding Rosa* won the 2009 Wilfrid Eggleston Award for Non-Fiction, the Bressani Prize for Writing about Immigration in 2010, and was shortlisted for the City of Edmonton Book Award. Edwards's most recent novel, *The Sicilian Wife*, was published by Linda Leith Publishing in 2015. *Caterina Edwards: Essays on Her Works*, edited by Joseph Pivato (Guernica, 2000), was the first in Guernica's Writers Series. Edwards is a member of the Writers' Guild of Alberta, the Canadian Creative Nonfiction Collective, the Writers' Union of Canada, and the Association of Italian Canadian Writers. For many years she taught creative writing at Grant MacEwan College, Athabasca University, and the University of Alberta. Edwards continues to reside in Edmonton and visited the Canadian Literature Centre for her Brown Bag Lunch reading on September 23, 2009.

4

CATERINA EDWARDS
History Lost in Forgetfulness

JOSEPH PIVATO

CATERINA EDWARDS'S BOOK *Finding Rosa* (2008) deals with the
themes that have dominated her novels, short stories, and essays: the
complexity and elusiveness of identity, both personal and ethnic, in
our world of mass migration. Closely connected to identity is the indi-
vidual's and society's relation to the past. Her first novel, *The Lion's
Mouth* (1982), has some basis in Edwards's life in Alberta and her trav-
els to Venice, Italy. The main character, Bianca, is a young woman who
must find her place as she grows up with split loyalties between the old
world and the new. We find many contrasts between Venice, the city of
canals and grand palaces, which represents the past, and Edmonton,
the prairie city on the river, which represents the present. The Venetian
politics of intrigue and betrayal are in contrast to the apparently trans-
parent politics of Edmonton. Despite the fame of Venice in art and
literature, Bianca realizes that as a woman and a writer, she has greater
creative freedom in the prairie city. Like the determined daughter in
Finding Rosa, Bianca is sometimes in conflict with the strong women in
her extended family.

Edwards's collection *Island of the Nightingales* (2000) has stories
set in Venice, Istria (Croatia), or Canada and all explore the effects of
migration and exile on the lives of women. These are themes to which
she returns to in *Finding Rosa*. Edwards's play, *Homeground* (1990), deals

with members of an immigrant family in Edmonton who plan to return to Italy with their circle of friends only to find that they no longer fit in back in the old country because it has changed as much as the Canadian experience has changed each of them. The characters illustrate how identity can shift without the person noticing that it is happening. When the play was first produced at the Edmonton Fringe Theatre festival it was titled *Terra Straniera*, which is Italian for *foreign land*. This original title is the opposite of the final English title, *Homeground*, and points to the changing perspectives in the play. The problem of shifting identity is taken up again in *Finding Rosa* by both the mother and the daughter.

In Edwards's novella *Becoming Emma* (1992), a young woman of Latvian origin struggles to establish herself as an abstract painter in an art world preoccupied with national identity and international notoriety. As in *Finding Rosa*, political conflict in Europe and exile in North America form the story's background. The many allusions to Jane Austen's *Emma* and Flaubert's *Madame Bovary* in this text refer to the many ways that personal identity can be constructed. Edwards is interested in exploring the particular complications of the search for identity of a woman and an artist.

Edwards's *Finding Rosa* is a work of creative nonfiction, which explicitly tries to uncover the truth about her mother's early life in Istria and Venice. This book has mystery, conflict, love, nostalgia, history, memory, and forgetting. The author has combined three storylines into one book. It is, first, the story of the turbulent life of Edwards's mother, Rosa, from the First World War to 2001. It is also the reconstructed history of the Italian refugees from Istria who lost their country at the end of the Second World War and became exiles all over the world. And it is the story of Edwards's own re-examined and troubled relationship with her mother, Rosa. These narrative strands are contained in the subtitle of *Finding Rosa: A Mother with Alzheimer's, a Daughter in Search of the Past*.

Unlike Edwards's other works of fiction, *Finding Rosa* is a memoir in which the author tries to reconstruct scenes and events in the real life of Rosa, a real person she has known all her life. All the relatives and friends we meet are real people whom she interviews in order to learn about the life and times of her mother. We should not confuse Rosa with a character in a novel or play, even though she might remind us of characters in Edwards's fictional works. It can be more difficult to write about a real person and the historical events in her life, since the author does not have the freedom to invent events and colourful characters.

As Edwards describes her, Rosa Pagan was a strong-willed person all her life. In the last four years of her old age she suffered from Alzheimer's disease and, like many people with this debilitating disease, she became difficult to care for. Nevertheless, Edwards, her husband, Marco, and their two daughters cared for this woman at home as she began to forget all of her long history and the story of her family and people. As a university student, Edwards had taken many trips back to Venice to visit her mother's remaining family. She was always troubled by unanswered questions. What had happened to her grandfather and why did the family leave the island of Lussino? Edwards began this book as a project on the history of Istria. She found that the years of research and trips back to Italy gradually helped her to better understand her mother and the troubled past of her family. She found that she could not write on Istria without writing about her mother as well. In this book we see that European history becomes personal, leaving scars for later generations—Edwards and Marco as well as their children are affected by events in Istria.

In recreating the very memorable history of her mother, Rosa, Edwards may have also come to better understand herself and her own history in Italy and Canada. The realism and emotion of this journey of discovery are deeply moving. We also learn about the buried history of hundreds of forgotten exiles, who were abandoned by their fellow Italians. Istria became part of Yugoslavia after the Second World War and hundreds of thousands of Italian nationals were forced to leave, but few were accepted back in Italy and so most had to go into exile as displaced persons. At the time Edwards was writing *Finding Rosa*, the Italian history of Istria was forgotten or denied. Coincidentally, since 2005, writers and journalists have begun to search out the truth about

Istria and publish their findings (see, e.g., Petacco; Pupo). We should remember that in the 1990s, Yugoslavia broke up in to separate states after years of civil war, and we once more witnessed thousands of displaced people and genocide, which is sometimes called ethnic cleansing. Here the war involved not just national identity but religion.

Rosa Pagan's Alzheimer's disease becomes a metaphor for the amnesia of national leaders of our own day who seem to have forgotten the evils of war. Every page of this book resonates with the history we have witnessed and with images similar to those we are seeing now in the trouble spots around the world. Edwards laments,

> My city does not conform to any actual Istrian city. It is a sequence of images and apprehensions that remains fixed in my mind. Over 85 percent of the population of the coastal cities did leave during the exodus. Capodistria, Rovigno, Pola, Zara, Parenzo, and Fiume, as they had been, disappeared. (276)

Italy is so full of history that it is hard to believe that any of it could be missing, erased and forgotten. Nevertheless, when you visit cities like Trieste, or Udine in Friuli, you sense a missing history. The story of the Italian Istrians is fragmented and forgotten. Records in the Dalmatian cities and towns listed above were destroyed by Tito's troops; even headstones in graveyards were defaced. Edwards had to contact Istrian exiles in Edmonton, Vancouver, Toronto, Montréal, New York, Seattle, Australia, Italy, and other distant places. Some, such as Toronto writer Gianni Grohovaz, died before she started her research project. It is a story that needs to be told of people who have disappeared. The work of Caterina Edwards is an attempt to rescue these people from oblivion. She ends her journey on a small hopeful note: "Her people were scattered to the four corners of the earth. And the culture—the last embers glowed in a club in Sydney, flickered in a restaurant in Long Island, flared bright in a kitchen in Seattle. And on the Istrianet Web" (323).

The excerpt from *Finding Rosa* reproduced in this anthology is from Chapter 7, which is entitled, "Them and Us," and tries to capture the perspective of Armida, an aged cousin of Edwards's mother, Rosa. As a young woman Armida married into a Croatian family but never learned Croatian and continued to speak Italian even after Istria became part of Yugoslavia. And even though she spent most of her life in Croatia and was married to a Croatian man, she still referred to Croatians as the other, thus her phrase "them and us." The passage illustrates how deeply ethnic identity reaches and how long it can last. It suggests that nationalist politics and feuds can go on for years and across generations. Armida, Maria Lettich, and their children personify this generational pattern.

On the language question, Armida explains that she did not want to speak her husband's Croatian dialect because it "sounded ugly to me," and was not proper Croatian. The language choices seem to go beyond Italian or Croatian since we note that Edwards and Armida are speaking the Istro-Veneto dialect. Armida only switches to standard Italian the next day when Marco accompanies Edwards to the interview. Identity and family ties are linked to regional dialects. For Armida, her distant Canadian cousin, Edwards, is one of "us," while her Croatian husband will always be one of "them."

In this chapter, cousins Maria Lettich and Armida distinctly recall long-ago details about their families and histories. This is in sharp contrast to the author's mother, Rosa, who is suffering from Alzheimer's disease and is slowly forgetting everything about herself, her family, her history, and in effect is losing her identity. Edwards is drawing a parallel between Rosa's disease and her fellow Istrians losing their history, being exiled from their very own identity.

In the passage, Edwards includes a reference to the Roman presence on the island of Lussino, then called Apsertides. In Greek mythology, the witch Medea killed her brother, Apsertides, to help Jason and the Argonauts escape her angry father: "The island of Apsertides was where a sister turned against her brother, where blood betrayed blood for a false love" (70). The reference is in keeping with the theme of personal and political betrayal that the people of Istria experienced in their history. Alzheimer's is also a personal betrayal of your own blood as your body and mind begin to deteriorate, leaving you trapped inside. We might ask, is there any "you" left after Alzheimer's, and is there any such place as Istria after cultural genocide?

By the end of her visit with Armida, Edwards realizes, once again, how her relatives' experiences in Istria and Italy have affected their views about modern European history and the truth about themselves. Edwards has collected versions of their stories in order to reconstruct the history of her family, a history lost in forgetfulness. By the end of the book, we ask questions about how personal identity is formed and can change. Caterina Edwards has salvaged stories about her family to better understand her mother and to better understand herself as a person, a daughter, a mother, and a writer. In the process, her nonfiction recaptures some of the lost history of Istria. A reader might ask, is our individual identity bound up with our region and nation? How can an artist navigate ethnic identity or the power of ideology?

Works Cited

Edwards, Caterina. *Finding Rosa: A Mother with Alzheimer's, a Daughter in Search of the Past.* Vancouver: Douglas & McIntyre, 2008. Print.

———. *Homeground: A Play.* Montréal: Guernica Editions, 1990. Print.

———. *Island of the Nightingales.* Toronto: Guernica Editions, 2000. Print.

———. *The Lion's Mouth.* Edmonton: NeWest Press, 1982. Print.

———. *A Whiter Shade of Pale* and *Becoming Emma.* Two Novellas. Edmonton: NeWest Press, 1992. Print.

Petacco, Arrigo. *A Tragedy Revealed: The Story of the Italian Population of Istria, Dalmatia and Venezia Giulia, 1943–1956.* Trans. Konrad Eisenbichler. Toronto: University of Toronto Press, 2005. Print.

Pupo, Raoul. *Il lungo esodo, Istria: le persecuzioni, le foibe, l'esilio.* Milano: Rizzoli Editore, 2005. Print.

Finding Rosa (excerpt)

ALTHOUGH THIRTY YEARS HAD PASSED, I didn't expect to find my mother's other cousin, Armida, so white haired and wrinkled. And from the way she hugged and kissed me and shook her head, I could tell that she too had expected my younger self. Several times as we caught up on family news, on my children and her grandchildren and on all the deaths (the list was long), Armida paused and gave me an appraising look. Finally she said, "You've put on the pounds and the years. Once, you were a flower."

Her comments on my lost youth bothered me not just because they were true but because I knew she would pass them onto her son, with whom I had once been infatuated (as enchanted with him as I'd been with Lussino). I did not point out how she had changed. I exclaimed over the house, which was no longer a fisherman's cottage but had been renovated and shone from top to bottom. "I didn't need this," Armida said, "Not now, when I'm old, but my son insisted. He comes as much as he can with his family."

"It's hard for me to go to him in Koper. It's another country now. It's Slovenia, there's a border, so it's off the bus and passports, then back on the bus. No, no. I'm too old. My legs." She brought me pictures of the grandsons to admire and a poem the oldest one had written in Italian, a hymn to the rocks and the sea of the island. "He won a prize," she said, "Boruth." Her mouth twisted.

"It took me years to learn how to pronounce it. Not one of our names. And then, I didn't plan it, but I was at the grocer's buying a little coffee—it wasn't so expensive then—he asked me about the new baby, and I said his name was Davide." Armida looked embarrassed. "Then I told everyone Boruth was Davide. Even Mario [her husband], may he rest in peace, called him Davide. Till that summer, my daughter-in-law was walking the baby and everyone came out and started making a fuss, calling him Davide. Then they made me call him Boruth—though I think they learned something, because they called the second one Leonardo."

I asked Armida, as I had asked Maria Lettich, on which side her father, my grandfather, had fought in the first war. "Austria," Armida said. "No, Italy. Who knows?" (Maria had not known either.) Armida and I were sitting on her terrace overlooking the inlet of Rovenska, rows of small white boats below us, a stretch of pine woods, then a sandy beach to the right, and ahead the stone jetty built by Archduke Maximilian, who went on to become the emperor of Mexico.

I pointed out that despite her Croatian husband and son, she spoke of them and us. "As far back as I can remember, it has always been them and us," she said. "We called them *Slavi*, and they called us *Chioggiotti*."

"Surely all the Italians weren't from Chioggia," I said, referring to the town on the edge of the Venetian lagoon.

"Maybe originally, hundreds of years ago."

"And lots didn't fit into them and us—some were Austrians and Hungarians." I had seen the censuses going back to 1880.

"We had separate dance halls." Armida continued. "And every now and then, there would be a big fight."

A rumble, I thought. "You never danced together? How did you start with your husband?"

"You're right. We would talk in the piazza. And then he started coming to our dances. I wasn't the only one. Oh no, there's always been lots of intermarriage."

Hard to keep them and us straight, I would have thought. But I said, "You never learned Croatian?" I tried not to sound disapproving.

"Everyone spoke our language, and by the time they didn't..."

"But marrying into a Croatian family?"

"I didn't want to. *Po nase*, their dialect sounded ugly to me. It isn't proper Croatian, you know."

"Neither is our language proper Italian."

"When I went to Rijeka to the clinic, the heart specialist and the nurses, they asked Antonio, how can it be that your mother doesn't speak Croatian? So he had to explain—how it used to be."

Circe was not the only witch associated with Lussino. In classical antiquity, until the Romans dug a canal at Osor, the islands of Cherso and Lussino were one island called Apsertides, for Apsyrtos, the brother of the witch Medea. The myth claimed that Medea killed her brother on this island and scattered his limbs across the sea to save Jason from her father. Medea knew that her father would stop and weep over his son's remains, and Jason and his Argonauts would be able to sail away. The island of Apsertides was where a sister turned against her brother, where blood betrayed blood for a false love.

| As soon as he felt better, Marco suggested we cut our trip short and go back to Venice. I was growing tired. Trying to discover the true nature of Losinj was making me feel as if I were a child again, straining to see through a white net and decipher the darkness beyond.

When I returned to Armida's with Marco, she chattered, though in Italian rather than Istro-Veneto, even more than the first time. "What can I offer you?" Fetching coffee and anise-seed cookies, uncorking a bottle of white wine, then one of pear brandy. Drink, eat, drink, drink, she said. "Isn't this a view?"

The three of us sat and stared at the curve of the bay, the blinding blue bordered by pale yellow sand. Beside and below us, on the surface, at least, a model of the fishing-port-turned-holiday-village: a scattering of small yachts, a restaurant awning barely covering the sprawl of tables on the quay, and spruced-up houses, plastered and painted, with green shutters and germanium-filled flower boxes. Armida had sprayed herself with the cologne we had bought her, and I was surrounded by the spicy, floral scent. And she brought out her grandson's poem again, this time so that Marco could read and admire it.

And she talked and talked. I prompted her with questions, but I avoided guiding her or putting words in her mouth. She wandered from memory to memory, doubling back at times, taking sudden turn-offs. The red and yellow sails on her father's boats, the cornmeal diet in the war, her heart condition. My mother when she was young, my grandmother when she was old, and me—what a bossy and articulate toddler I was.

She complained that she couldn't get good coffee in Losinj, that her pension did not arrive for months at a time, that she was alone. Oh, her husband's family checked on her, cooked for her if she wasn't well. Like Maria, she didn't go to church anymore: on Sundays, she stayed home and watched the mass on TV in Italian. Antonio had got her a satellite dish, so she got all the Italian channels.

"I hardly know anyone anymore. The town is full of strangers. Your mother is lucky that she lives with you and that you take care of her."

"I don't think she realizes." I felt a twinge of guilt. I flashed to my mother, who was in respite care at the General Continuing Care Hospital during my absence. I saw her bibbed and belted into her wheelchair, her eyes confused, lost.

Armida flipped back to 1950, when her husband was taken away for three months of forced labour. Everyone had to go. Then the soldiers with the red star on their caps came to her door and told her she had no right to be here. She must be gone in twenty-four hours. She was married, five months pregnant. At least the soldiers didn't come in the night, as they did for some. Some people would say they weren't worried—their consciences were clear—then you'd never see them again. Someone had denounced them. A neighbor who coveted their land, we used to think. Or someone they had crossed maybe years before. It was a time of revenge.

"What did you do?" Marco asked.

"Luckily, my husband's family had some connections who produced the right papers."

"False papers?" I asked.

She shrugged. "I became officially a Croat." (Slavicized, Italianized, people here had been shifting, changing their identities, for at least a hundred years. Your proclaimed nationality depended on convenience or, if times were good, on your vision of yourself.)

"You're sure," she said as I wrote in my notebook, "that no one here will read what I say?" When I had phoned her from Hotel La Punta, when I'd told her I would like her to talk about her life, she'd been surprised: "Why do you want to know?" And now she continued to ask me, "Who will see what you write? Will anyone here know?"

I reassured her yet again. "I'm sure no one here will see it. Here or in Italy." Thinking of the number of books I had sold the previous year: "And not many in North America. I'll change your name if that makes you feel better."

"That won't fool them. They'll know who I am."

I thought she was paranoid, but she had lived her life under Fascism and then Communism, and I had not. Despite her fears, however, she was elated by this chance to tell her story. And her excitement fueled her words. "What else do you want me to tell you? What else do you want to know?"

What else? I was waiting for a revelation: the meaning of her life in this place. More, I was waiting, wanting, to capture what was hidden behind the stone walls, inside the silent, locked villas, under the crumbling roofs. A dark truth like truffles clustered on the roots of oak trees, like spores infesting the blood-coloured earth. A luminous truth like the darting, dancing light of the phosphorescence in Rovenska Bay. The truth now and the truth then. *Once.* The word echoed in my head: *once.*

The mix of wine and bitter coffee left me lightheaded. "Mario made lots of money ferrying those who left," Armida was saying. "For months, he sailed to Italy, his boat overloaded. I was afraid the whole time that he'd capsize. You wouldn't believe what people tried to take with them."

The local representatives of the Yugoslav government would not allow the exiles to take anything deemed of value: money, jewelry, paintings, Turkish rugs, or Chinese porcelain. Nor many objects of emotional worth: books, an accordion, a record player, a demijohn of wine, a drum of olive oil, a plow, a shovel, a scythe, a lantern, a sewing machine, wool-stuffed mattresses, wooden chairs, feather comforters, copper pots, dishes, silver rubbed with dirt and ashes so that it looked like tin, a bicycle. A mountain of things were abandoned on the quay, surrendered because there was no room in the boats.

"Mario took my parents and then each of my brothers to Trieste. Silvio and Miro—I never saw them again." For the first time, Armida sounded old and tremulous.

As the sun set, in that round red ball of a moment, I could feel the fear of those in the boats, the urge to flee, abandoning possessions, homes, family, sailing away from their lives, their language, their ancestors who had been always with them in the earth under their feet. The past, their past, was gone. On sailboats and fishing boats and ferries, in carts driven by oxen, in the military trucks the Americans had left behind, night after night for months, for years, they fled the towns, the islands, the mainland cities. And those who remained—they too were afraid, walking the deserted streets, stunned and alone. And they too—though they never left their homeland—they too lost it.

I feel I am a stranger in my own country...the wrong kind of Italian.
An Italian-Istrian poet, Quarantotti Gambini, in an interview

The next morning, I gave in. We would cut the trip short and leave the following day. I had wanted to check the archives in Mali Losinj for records of my grandparents, but Maria Lettich had explained that the old archives, like those of most of the towns in Istria, had all been burned in a supposedly accidental fire. Both she and Armida insisted that the priest would never let me see the parish records.

We took a final tour of the graveyard behind the church overlooking the sea. Neither of my grandparents was buried there, but I wanted to see the graves of both Zia Cecilia and Zia Giuditta. The graveyard was austere: no trees and only one family chapel. A drystone wall marked the circumference. The paths were beaten red earth, the headstones grey marble or white stone. There was a small oval picture of Zia Cecilia on her headstone, hair white but thick, chin up, earrings dangling. On her grave, a circle of white lilies. Again, I wished I had asked her questions when I'd had the chance.

The dates on the stones went back several hundred years. In some graveyards, during the time of the *foibe*, the Italian names were chipped out of the headstones; here they were unmolested. Back and back, a Ragusin married a Gladofich, a Penso married a Siminich, a Lanza and a Barcèvic, a Lettich and a Pagan.

Everyone I had spoken to before I had come to Losinj and since I had been here made clear divisions: exiles and *Rimasti*, Slavs and *Chioggiotti*, real Lussignani and new settlers, Italians, Croats, Serbs, and lately, Bosnians. Them and us—but here in the graveyard one category merged into the next.

The house where my mother was born was across the road from the one where Maria Lettich lived. At the end of my second visit, she and I stood outside the tall green gate and rang the bell. "Once," Maria said, beginning a story I had heard before. "Once, there was an orange tree in your grandparents' garden, and that led to their name in Lussino, Ponaronzo. Those of the orange tree." When no one answered, with Maria's encouragement, I unlatched the gate and stepped into the garden.

The house looked solid, secure and substantial. But it was eclipsed by the magnificent tree that stretched taller than the roof. Nestled in the green shiny leaves were small, bright bitter oranges. Once there was an orange tree? Once? Still. This time the word was still. Even if the family had changed. Or could this be another tree? A replacement or an offspring?

I see children, my aunts and uncles, under the boughs of the tree. Two of the boys wrestle, howling, rolling back and forth over the roots. The oldest girl, Maricci, tries to reprimand them. She has a book open on her lap. Enea—I recognize her immediately; even as a child she has a big nose—Enea dangles a baby on her hip. A toddler is trying to cram an entire unpeeled orange into his mouth.

I look back at the silent, shuttered house. In a bedroom on the second floor, I see my grandmother, her black hair soaked in sweat, her face twisted in pain. The shutters are open; the sunlight pours in across the bloodied sheets, the matrimonial bed. She is laboring to deliver her seventh child. Stoically, her lips are

clamped shut, but the midwife talks and the mother-in-law prays. Finally, the
baby, who was turned the wrong way, has righted herself and is coming. Now her
scream penetrates the window, tosses the leaves and branches. The children stop;
each one of them looks up.

This place is where my mother began.

Memories and stories—mine and my mother's and my aunts',
the memoirs I have read, the exiles' newsletters, the Internet post-
ings. Memories and stories—two glowing ropes that intertwine and
separate, slip by each other and knot over the dark pit, the *foiba* of
forgetfulness.

MARINA ENDICOTT may be well known in theatre circles, but it is as an author of fiction that she has received widespread attention for her gripping and uncompromising look at life, both through a modern and a historical lens. She was born in Golden, British Columbia, in 1958 and grew up in Vancouver, Halifax and Yarmouth, and Toronto. After graduating from Bishop Strachan School in Toronto in 1978, Endicott attended and earned a degree in acting from the University of Waterloo. In 1982, Endicott left Canada to pursue theatre in London, England. While there, she drafted short stories that would go on to be published in *Coming Attractions* (Oberon, 1994). Endicott returned to Canada in 1984, where she took up a post in Saskatoon, Saskatchewan, as the dramaturge of the Saskatchewan Playwright's Centre. It was while living in Saskatchewan that she published her first short story, "Being Mary," in *Grain Magazine* (1985). By 1993, Endicott had seen a short story, "With the Band," shortlisted for the 1993 Journey Prize. After relocating to Mayerthorpe, Alberta, Endicott worked for six months in 1997 at the local newspaper, which provided her with one of the few outlets for writing available in the area. In 2001, Endicott's first novel, *Open Arms* (Douglas & McIntyre, 2001; Freehand Books, 2009) was shortlisted for the Amazon.ca/*Books in Canada* First Novel Award and was adapted for CBC Radio's *Between*

the Covers broadcast in 2003. In 2006, Endicott's long poem, "The Policeman's Wife, Some Letters," written about the Mayerthorpe RCMP shooting tragedy, was shortlisted for the CBC Literary Awards. Her second novel, *Good to a Fault* (Freehand Books, 2008), about the double-edged sword of caring, was awarded the regional Commonwealth Writers' Prize (Canada and the Caribbean), and was also shortlisted for the Scotiabank Giller Prize and longlisted for the IMPAC Dublin Literary Award. The *Globe and Mail* also recognized *Good to a Fault* as one of their Top 100 Books for 2008. In 2011, Endicott released a book titled *New Year's Eve* in collaboration with ABC Life Literacy Canada as part of their Good Reads book series written for adult literacy learners. That year also saw the publication of her third novel, *The Little Shadows* (Doubleday, 2011), which was longlisted for the Scotiabank Giller Prize and a finalist for the Governor General's Award for English-language fiction. In 2012, Endicott co-wrote the screenplay for the National Film Board of Canada documentary *Vanishing Point. Close to Hugh*, Endicott's humorous and compassionate fourth novel, about a man compelled to ease the pain of those around him, was published by Doubleday in 2015. Endicott has worked as a creative writing instructor at the University of Alberta, the Canadian Mennonite University, and in 2014 was the Toronto Reference Library's Writer-in-Residence. Her writing has also been published in *Joyland* and *Alberta Views*. Endicott splits her time between Edmonton and Toronto and is presently at work on her fifth novel. She visited the Canadian Literature Centre twice to read at the Brown Bag Lunch, first on November 18, 2009, and again on November 14, 2012.

5

MARINA ENDICOTT
Lights and Shadows across the Continent

DANIEL LAFOREST

THERE IS A LIGHT SHINING through Marina Endicott's four books. This is not exactly a metaphor. Her writing captures a sense of being together in the world, whether we're alone or not, under vast expanses of skies, while the late afternoon light descends and makes every aspect of the scenery somewhat more palpable, more *there*. Elsewhere, in less capable hands, such a setting would impart ordinary melancholy or a form of longing. Not with Endicott. Not in *Open Arms* (2001), in *Good to a Fault* (2008), in *The Little Shadows* (2011), or in *Close to Hugh* (2015), to say nothing of her short stories, which were anthologized in the 1990s. Throughout each of her thematically varied novels, Endicott has perfected a unique craft in which a grand, sweeping narrative carrying the fate of individuals and families seems rooted, even if just for a moment, in a minute interplay of light and shade that contains the emotional substance of North American life.

Despite this aesthetics of peace or dreamy contemplation, Endicott's writing deploys a vast array of tormented emotions resulting from often misguided actions in characters whose lives appear to escape their control. She is a master of literary realism and the emotional complexity of the mind embracing the geographical expanses of a world as beautiful as it is indifferent. Perhaps therein lies the reason for the oft-noted compassion of Endicott's writing. Maybe such a true, fearless love of the country (in a deep, non-national sense of the word) explains the warmth and the human closeness emanating from her novels. Or perhaps the light I've mentioned is more like a wind, or like a breath, as the titles of her books suggest. There are the "open arms" of close bodily contact as well as the human-size "shadows" of women cut out against the prairie sky. And with *Close to Hugh*, the readers themselves are invoked by the emotional interplay of a novel whose title could refer to its protagonist just as much as to its author's relationship to her readership. Human closeness, its memory or its potential, is the wind that *breathes* through all of Endicott's novels. Characters may be moving about a geography that is larger than they will ever be, but they are not wanderers in the wilderness. Nor are they lost souls in the crowd. They are drawn to and move toward each other.

A *deus ex machina* in an Impossibly Vast Country

A majority of characters in Endicott's fiction are travellers. Their favoured terrain, like that of the author herself, is the Canadian Prairies. This does not prevent them from sometimes veering toward the United States as a land of uncertain opportunities, like in *The Little Shadows*, or toward the nondescript North where work in compressed shifts lures the despaired family at the beginning of *Good to a Fault*. But the reader will notice a kind of *deus ex machina* encompassing the novels and providing a drastic counterbalance to this revised call of the wild favoured by Endicott: randomness strikes and accidents happen. Fate in the world of Endicott is certainly blind but that is not what makes it interesting or for that matter endearing. The car accident that opens *Good to a Fault* and the burlesque fall taken by Hugh Argylle in *Close to Hugh* set the tone for these two novels, while preventing their characters from going much further concretely and figuratively. The disenfranchised family of *Good to a Fault* loses their last possession—precisely their mode of locomotion, the car in which they were living—and the ensuing drama revolves around the place where fate struck. *Close to Hugh* offers the rare literary treat of a comedy that contemplates the potential unraveling of a busy mind in places like a hospice or a hospital. The reader laughs nervously. He knows his mind is held hostage within the suspended time opened by an accident that in theory is absurd but that for anyone interested in the mastery of the novelistic structure is all but random.

Endicott is interested in exploring how ordinary people come together through accidents of fate that are, in and of themselves, also ordinary. This is one of the most difficult feats for a novelist. The couple in the short story "New Year's Eve" is on the road. A blizzard forces them to leave the highway. Such a Canadian experience! But only in its wake do significant human encounters happen. Only then does life find meaning and the story its raison d'être. The three sisters of *The Little Shadows* are exposed to the mercurial moods of the inscrutable vaudeville entertainment world in which they have been thrown at an early age. A bad audition, a yes or a no, can alter the course of everything. Outside in the unfathomable distance, the First World War is raging. Heroes are either exceptional or the product of exceptional circumstances. But car collisions like the one in *Good to a Fault* happen every day in North America. And a cruel case can be made about the ordinariness of entire families turning homeless "in this economy," as the current media have become prone to say in recent years. Endicott has control over the narrative fate she instills in her stories; she makes equally sure that such fate will not devolve into maudlin endings where resolution is offered to the reader at the expense of verisimilitude. The characters in Endicott's novels are not heroes. They truly are ordinary. Which is to say it can be quite painful, or revelatory, for us to open a book by Endicott. She has a mastery of the minute emotions that come and go in people's heart when they find themselves in difficult situations that lead them to wonder what others would do in their place. This self-consciousness often turns into guilt, or resentment, of even hatred. On occasion, it can also become love.

Families and Fate

Be it at the dawn of the twentieth century in *The Little Shadows* or during the contemporary times of her other stories, world history does not hold the foreground. But history is not absent from the novels either. There, again, lies a distinctive trait of Endicott's mastery of the realist novel: history only matters when it passes through, or when it is reflected on, the smaller time spans of character's lives, joys, and turpitudes. The grand historical events do not power Endicott stories, although they are not entirely absent. They are diffracted amid the characters' emotions and actions. Hence the aforementioned economic doldrums of the late 2000s that set the scene in *Good to a Fault*, a story where selfishness is but the flipside of the self-proclaimed good intentions of Canadian civility, and where money and the fear of lacking it explain far too many things in the end. A woman bluntly wants to steal the children of another woman, under the pretense that she is helping this mother who cannot provide for her own family. But human relations are never that simple. It is never exactly clear if *Good to a Fault*'s main character, Clara, is aware of her own failings. Nor is it clear if Bella, the most driven sister in *The Little Shadows*, knows of the proverbial shadow she can cast on others. A simple linear analysis of character development in Endicott's novels would not bear fruitful results. The biographical milestones through which we, the readers, measure a character's destiny and enjoy our identification to it are not sufficient. The main lesson of the rich worlds Endicott conveys is that for all their fictional nature her characters feel real to us: comprehension and eventual acceptance of our own fate only comes with the small actions and the tiny shifts of the heart that seem to take place in the interstices of time. Time in turn can reveal the extent to which the uncontrollable forces of history are reflected in the existences of those who, like Endicott's characters, have chosen very little of the human turmoil in which they find themselves.

The all-feminine cast of Endicott's first novel *Open Arms*, and especially the young Bessie Smith Connolly, offer the best example of all that precedes. Fate is something no one chooses. But it exists, insofar as stories exist. Fate, or at the very least its impression, its *sense*, is what the novels of Endicott recreate for their reader. Her characters alone are incapable of grasping it, just like they are incapable of controlling the very North American continental pull that set them in motion in the first place and often sends them adrift on the roads like the *saltimbanques* (or entertainers) of old times who are the ancestors of contractual artists in the world of contemporary theatre from which Endicott often draws. This is why deeper readings of Endicott's books will reveal various forms of community at play in her literary world. The first one, of course, is the family. It is central to every novel. However, to say that Endicott's families are "broken" would be to diminish the spectrum through which that theme is exposed in her works. Families themselves are never alone in the novels. Civic institutions surround them and, somehow, give them a different face than what is commonly expected. In other words, families in the novels of Endicott, while the driving force of the narrative, never function in closed quarters. Just look at Hugh in the passage reproduced in this anthology: Endicott has bended her otherwise precise language to reflect that character's brush with the mental alienation of a major life crisis. The fact that the novel comes across as this author's funniest (there is real competition, with *Open Arms* especially) is telling. When surrounded by others, a character's pain, however far-reaching, will first take the form of a drama in its purest Greek sense: something to be experienced by an audience, and in which emotions will always potentially attain a universal quality.

Being Alive and a Reader in Canada

Is there a link between Endicott's fiction and her life as an actor and playwright, along with her profound knowledge of the theatre world? I would suggest caution to anyone wanting to go down that route. There certainly is a relation. But all the world is not always a stage. The novel as Endicott practices it, with its aforementioned engagement with history, the human condition, Canadian geography, and the underrepresented daily problems of ordinary citizens caught in the immense emotions of petty quarrels, is different from what goes on in drama or stage writing. In fiction, language has to play with time and space far more than with dialogues or confrontations. *The Little Shadows* exemplifies this. It ranks among the most accomplished Canadian novel set in the world of entertainment, and provides a vintage version of it at that. But it is also a novel about what goes on between three women tied together by blood, ambition, the vagaries of the entertainer's life in a world that engulfs them, and as elsewhere a well-intentioned but feeble mother character. The amount of unexpressed emotions in Endicott's writing is vertiginous. Yet the novel makes us *feel* them. How? Because Endicott understands something all great writers understand: our truest feelings are inevitably our secret, unconscious, and often shameful feelings, the ones that language can only tiptoe around or paraphrase. Endicott has a deep trust in her readers. She knows deep down that they will accept to follow the uneasy road, the one that starts with compassion, runs through joy and sadness, and ends in the realization that being alive means awaiting another story instead of closure.

Works Cited

Marina Endicott. *Close to Hugh*. Toronto: Doubleday Canada, 2015. Print.

——. *Good to a Fault*. Calgary: Freehand Books, 2008. Print.

——. *The Little Shadows*. Toronto: Doubleday Canada, 2011. Print.

——. *New Year's Eve*. Toronto: GoodReads/HarperCollins, 2011. Print.

——. *Open Arms*. Toronto: Douglas & McIntyre, 2001. Print.

Close to Hugh (excerpt)

MONDAY

Oh, the Hughmanity

dukkha, *suffering,*
or better, a basic unsatisfactoriness
that pervades all of life.

> *entry on Buddhism,*
> WIKIPEDIA

You can bear pain. Hugh can. But you can't stand to see it in others. It
makes your hands and feet hurt. The grey room is full of grey people in
various stages of pain. A little party: grouped by the window, sitting on
the bed, ten or twelve of them. A woman kneeling by the nightstand
says, *It's all up to you, up to Hugh.* Her cloudy hair, her dress in tatters. No.

No. It's a dream.

Eyes open.

Light? No. Three a.m. 3:02.

Okay.

3:07.

Hugh can bear pain. For himself it's not so bad, sometimes he
doesn't even notice it. Hard when it's someone you can't help, though.
Your mother. Cloudy hair all wisps and tendrils now. No. Don't think
about Mimi, her hands, the pale phosphorescent skin of her chest, her
searching eyes.

If you had a child, could you stand that? There's a question for you,
for Hugh: why didn't you have a child? Okay, Ann had that abortion in
the eighties. But that was somebody else's baby, Hugh is pretty sure. By
then Ann was disconnecting herself from him by connecting with a
few other people. You couldn't blame her, it was the times; women felt
they had to be libertines in order to be liberated, and there was a fair
amount of cocaine going around. He walked in on Ann once, having
sex with some guy on a pile of coats at a party. Humiliating, titillating,
to see her riding a set of naked limbs. Lots of reasons for shame. Hugh
never even saw who it was—the guy pulled a coat over his face against
the sudden light, and Hugh turned and left. That tawdry little pain hits
again, a bee-sting of stupidity.

Why remember things at all.

Hugh lies in the dark, listening to the night's last rain falling
straight into the basement of the gallery he lives above. Where valuable
things are stored, furniture and boxes he ought to have moved, other
people's art. He's tired of rain and basements and responsibility.

Della and Ken for dinner on Saturday, with Ruth—he should ask Newell too, but can't bear the burden of Burton, Newell's house guest. Della and Ken: that's a mess.

Think of something else: what to make for Ruth? Trivial, tepid, time-taking thought, a treat for old Ruth. She likes seafood crêpes. Okay, not rolled, but stacked like layer-cake. Frozen crab, not that reeking stuff from the truck they had last time. *Fresh? Liars!* said Ruth.

The first time he was sent to live with her, four years old, confused, he thought they said to call her Aunt Truth. Newell waiting with him, waiting for their mothers to come back: two boys side by side at the long white table, watching Ruth laugh as she stood stirring at the stove, laughing at something Jasper said. Jasper flirting in his peacocky shirt, gesturing with his glass—he didn't even drink too much, back then. When was that? 1969. Warm and safe in Ruth's foster-kitchen, those boys, backs against fake ivy-covered bricks on washed-clean vinyl wallpaper. Ivy in pots too, growing, growing, shining green, kind and clean.

Almost asleep again, Hugh wakes. Clean towels, nobody lying, nobody angry, nobody going off the rails. Della waiting with them too, the next year, after her mother's breakdown. At the kitchen table, Della making a sandwich: square cheese, square white bread. The only thing she would eat at Ruth's. That time, anyway.

Ken didn't float into view till they were in university. Floating out again now? Doozy of an anniversary dinner, if so.

Yesterday at their house, Della was playing the piano. Hugh's mother's piano, already moved out of what will be, has to be—what turns out to have been her last apartment.

No. Go back. Yesterday, Hugh stood at the bottom of the short flight of stairs in Ken and Della's front hall, listening. Suspended rippling phrases. Schumann? Getting good again, now she has Mimi's Steinway. Della staring at the music, head tilted; the face of a dear horse, the same since childhood. From that low angle through the banisters, he could see her daughter, Elle, lying under the grand piano, painting Della's toenails with bright pink polish.

His empty life. Della and her daughter.

The woman and her little son; the funeral in the morning.

Hugh has pretty much stopped sleeping. He naps in the evening, put down by half a bottle of wine; wakes at midnight. Up for a few hours, naps again around four a.m. The phone alarm shouts him up at six. Every morning he thinks, behind glued-shut eyelids, you should change that setting. Every morning he lies there saying no, no. You have to get up.

There's the gallery to attend to.

At night the apartment above the gallery is a ship in fog, a Swiss Family Robinson treehouse. Wooden shelves and floors, plank deck stretched out over the framing room roof at the back, overhung by trees. In the early morning it's a form of tree-burial, and he gets out fast.

The espresso machine stands by the sink in the framing room. He gimps down the back stairs on stiff bare feet, pokes the button. A grinding noise. The red light blinks: out of water. Always something. The stupid thing cost more than a fridge, and now he has to keep filling it up. He takes the latte (milk only faintly sour) to his desk and sits staring at the earth's crust of bills, papers, orders. Dusty red files with pathetic labels like **NOW!** or DO THIS WEEK.

He has to get moving. At least get dressed. The sun has come out. At FairGrounds, the coffee shop next door, a shining young girl is whacking mats against the porch post, sending dust whirling up into a devil. Della's Elle? Or one of the friends. She can't see into the gallery, he hasn't turned on the lights. But he can see her shadow perfectly: a perfect shadow. Elle, yes. Aureole of pale hair in sunrise, sunrays. Another one joins her—they lean on the railing, nymphs just out of the larval stage. The other one is dark, makes Elle look like a negative. Savannah—no, this one's Nivea, Nevaya, something invented—it's Nevaeh (middle name Lleh ha ha). One kisses the other's cheek. Their limbs are long like the lines of broom and rail. Diagonals, perpendiculars.

Della will be in soon to thrash out the text for January's class poster. Kids' classes, et cetera, *Introduction to Watercolours.* Okay, but Ian Mighton's collage master class starts next week—get the flyer finished for that.

Hugh himself is doing *Self-Portrait*, again.

And the funeral is at ten.

Well, that's okay, he hardly knew the woman. The little boy, though. Sad.

The empty room, the cup in front of him, his feet on the worn boards, the blinding window hiding him safe from view, his hermit shell upstairs: Hugh feels dizzy, as if the building is his mind, as if the whole world around him—the dead woman and her little son, Mighton coming, Della's Elle, non-Elle Nevaeh—all these who ought to be tangible are only instances of his ingenious mind inventing ways to occupy itself.

Last night until it rained he lay out on the deck above the framing room, wrapped in the old afghan Ruth made, under shifting shadows of branches, imagining a painting he will never paint. He can still see, or sense, it: the scale of it, the intricacy of the thinking. But he will not be able to execute it in paint or in collage, or by the xeroxing of the great.

The coffee is gone, it's eight. Get dressed. Grey tie, jacket.

Ruth's stomp on the front step, her key in the lock. Hugh is already hidden, hurrying halfway up the stairs. Can't bring himself to call out good morning.

| The funeral, okay. Time to go. Here's Della, climbing the gallery steps in her good black coat, bright paisley lining firmly unrevealed. Sober, not distressed; black chiffon wrapped round her neck, black hair bound up above it. Fine funereal turnout, for someone they hardly knew. Two years of Saturday parent/child painting classes—the mother seemed very nice.

"Such a bright little spark, Toby," Della says. "He'd try anything. Not even five yet. Never minded glue on his hands, as some do." Her expressive face falls into a clowning sadness, but not to mock. She pulls her coat sleeve across the morning-dusty counter, then slaps at the sleeve. "Ken can't come—he's team-building, a couple of days rappelling down Elora Gorge or some fool thing."

Uncomfortable, knowing more than she does, Hugh doesn't answer.

He flips the sign to *Back Soon* and locks the door. Ruth has run over to the Mennonite Clothes Closet to check on the coat she wants; they'll go on ahead. It's okay, there are no customers.

"How did Gerald find them, did you hear?" Della asks Hugh as they go stride for stride.

"Ruth says he came home from work and opened the garage door as usual. The groceries were still in the back of the car. Melted ice cream."

"She never seemed anything but cheerful, in class."

Hugh tries to remember the woman. Brown hair, worried eyes, a tidy little bundle in the back of the classroom, a fond hand on her son's head.

"They were old," Della says. "She was nearly fifty. They tried for ages to have Toby, Gerald told me once. He looks terrible, I saw him in Lucky Foods yesterday, wandering the aisles."

"Ruth cleaned for them—she says it was post-partum, only it never stopped."

"Gerald had no idea, none in the world."

"You know him outside of class?"

"We bought the car from him last year, I guess that counts. And he came to class, about half the time. He was so proud of the shared parenting thing. She's from—she was from Iowa. Missed her family, maybe? Or just tired of always coping..."

They turn up Oak Street.

Della slides her hand through Hugh's arm. "It might have been an accident...She gets home from shopping and stops for a little nap, forgetting all about carbon monoxide. I did it myself, when Elly was little—sat in the car for a while when we got home, because she was asleep and I knew if I took her out of the carseat she'd wake up and start crying. We just didn't have a garage to get gassed in—"

She breaks off as they join a small stream of walkers funnelling into the churchyard. Leaning closer to Hugh, she whispers: "He was such a nice little boy. Not difficult at all."

Inside the church Gerald lurches down the aisle, huge in a grey suit, the too-friendly salesman's cheer ironed out of his eyes. Sedated, Hugh supposes.

Gerald kisses Della's cheek, shakes hands. "It would mean so much to her that Hugh came," he tells Della.

Hooked on his own name, Hugh's ear checks, then fixes his error: the poor man only said "that *you* came."

But his mind sticks on it as he follows Della along a pew. How much would it mean to her? Did she close the garage door thinking, *This will be good, Hugh will come. They'll all come to the church, Gerald will be such a great host...*

Stop. They don't know that she did it on purpose. Maybe she was just tired. Drove into the garage and dozed; didn't sit there thinking, I can't, I cannot do this any more. Maybe she was not in terrible, terrible pain, the kind of pain that cannot be endured, the kind that you beg your son for release from, over and over.

(DELLA)

over the lawn beside the gallery (last shadows of last leaves shudder in
    small wind, ashes) will they burn the boy's body? (small ash grit)
into FairGrounds, say hi to Elly
(my mother's twelve identical canvases lined up around the room,
    strict economical palette, fishing boat after boat after boat after boat
    after boat after boat after boat after boat boat boat boat—is that
    twelve yet?—maybe the boats paid the mortgage, who knows how
    they managed,
Dad sad in the Barcalounger all night, unable to shift or go up the stairs)
                              at least Elly never has that to deal with
sad smell of his clothes the pity of him   eyes closed in the late afternoon
a cup of tea for his throat with whiskey in it
can't even look at poor old Jasper now   close my eyes against it
    nothing could have made me close Elly's eyes for ever, nothing
Elly at the counter, who loved me more than anything,
nothing in her eyes for me now

how can love be gone, that giant ardent unbearable passionate love,
 gone? the light in her face under the skin when she talks with
 Nevaeh, smiling as
she pulls the lever, the scream of the frother covering what she says
turn away so as not to read her lips, she deserves a private life
how rough a time she's having—is the pain only from living, the pity of
 it, or from some failing of mine or Ken's?
dear love, the mouth tugging at the breast and smiling, dancing in the
 bedroom, nothing sweeter, so open between us that it could never
 be closed
and yet here it is, gone
(hollow piece under the breastbone, how to do that in clay? how to get
 at that pocket of air there...identical, symmetrical, twelve boats, hull
 and prow laid down in a figure eight, pencil on blue-washed canvas,
 paint in patches, paint-by-number, torn postcard)
                              and Ken—where is he really? has he left us?
never mind never mind
if he is gone I will have the bed to myself and my thoughts
what passes for thoughts
nothing in my head but eyes

Hugh lives his life in the second person, never quite sure whether it's *Hugh* or *you*. Either one demands, accuses, requires responsibility. You'll do it—or was that Hugh'll do it? You/Hugh said everything would be okay. Why did you leave? Where did Hugh go?

It works the other way, too. Ruth, who works mornings as the gallery assistant (ostensibly so Hugh can spend time at the hospice), answers the phone on speaker, and a man's voice says, "May I speak to you?"

"Go right ahead," she says. A short silence. "Who's that?" she asks.

"Uhh, Mark, from the Ace?"

"Well, how can we help you?"

"I'm looking for Hugh?"

"Oh! I thought you said *you*." Ruth laughs to herself as she moves to the window to yell out to Hugh. He is listening from the porch, where he's been untangling strings of firefly lights he thought might brighten up the gallery sign.

The Ace Grill wants their staff awards certificates framed, Mark has a few concerns; Hugh will pick up the certificates, and can you get them done by...? Yes, Hugh can, for Saturday, for sure. The yellowing cream plastic of the receiver is heavy in his hand. The phone is almost as old as Ruth is. It's after noon already, and she only works mornings. She's getting her coat on, an old navy pea jacket. She pulls a red knitted hat out of the pocket. Still only October, but she is always cold. Her eyes are huge behind her glasses. He loves and is irritated by her in almost equal halves. He is stuck with her.

Trotting off for the day's second visit to the Clothes Closet, she calls back, "You be careful!" Old bat. Hugh taps his teeth together gently to keep from growling. Alternating sides, a bit OCD. His teeth are hurting. He has to shake off this bad temper.

He reaches to hook the lights over the sign, steps up to the next rung of the ladder, and misses it.

His foot slams down on nothing.

He falls.

Twenty feet, a long time—down onto a slumped bank of cedar chips. Lies on his back, stars (look, pointy stars!) circling in his vision. When he closes his eyes he sees op art, distorted checkerboards melting into Dali, so he opens them again.

Wind bellowed out of him, he lies there, unable to gasp for the longest time. It becomes clear, in a sunburst of cheap pop epiphany, that he has been this way his whole life: unable to breathe, lying as still as possible to avoid pain.

An ant on a leaf of grass in front of his opened eye, clouds in the baby blue sky, small people and their children going about the streets on their little paths like ants: all of them in pain all their lives, all dying. Mimi is in the hospice, Ruth on her way to the Clothes Closet. How the clouds too can be in pain he does not trouble to sort out.

Then his ribs creak open like a rusted umbrella and the blood comes drumming into his ears and eyes. A stroke? Fiftyish, he's about due. Nobody comes to help—nobody could have seen him fall from the ladder perched at the end of the porch.

For five or ten minutes he lies alone, dying or not dying, in a lot of pain. Then he gets up and puts the ladder in the shed again. Never mind the lights for now.

His head buzzes or blanks, something electrical wrong in there—he cannot stop thinking about Ruth, out of all the people around him who tremble on the edge of falling, ladders poised over the abyss, nobody to notice when they fall. Ruth, who should not be living alone on the OAS. He does her taxes, he knows she doesn't have enough money even with what he pays her at the gallery (two hundred a week for five mornings so he can go to the hospice; she's up early anyway) and the occasional cleaning job. She won't take his advice, clear out her cluttered house and move into an apartment. She wants to stay independent. Which she's not, anyway; she's entirely dependent on him continuing to hire her and pay her, even though she can never remember to say "Argylle Gallery" when she answers the goddamned phone. She is not an ideal employee.

But the fall is forcing empathy upon him. As he hangs the *Back Soon* sign in the window he figures out—and this is a real epiphany—that if she moved into a pleasant apartment with less stuff and less to worry about, she would actually be pre-dead.

He should be picking up the certificates from the Ace. But here he goes instead, ducking into the Mennonite Clothes Closet.

The trotting tassel of Ruth's red hat moves through close-packed aisles on the other side of the store. She plans to offer them less than the posted price for a corduroy jacket that has caught her fancy. She's been checking it every day. Hasn't quite worked up her nerve to suggest $5 instead of $15. "Strictly speaking," she told Hugh this morning, "I do not need a jacket. My navy peacoat's still good—*that* was a find— but the coppery tone, this wide-wale corduroy, just matches one I had when I was a girl, and I've got my wanter turned up loud."

No good for Hugh to buy it for her. She would whip out her little purse (pouched pink leather, like her mouth) and pay him back.

So he sidles down the aisles outside her narrowed peripheral vision, as she pretends to look everywhere but at the jackets. While she examines shoes, Hugh slips a sharp-edged, brown hundred dollar bill into the left-hand pocket of the corduroy jacket, from the opposite side of the musty-smelling rack. Ducks along behind the racks and out of the store.

Watching from the gallery he is rewarded, ten minutes later, by her squat copper-clad torso swanning along George Street, on her way home. Beyond his hope, he sees her shove her hands into the pockets. He can almost hear the crinkle. She pulls her left hand out, and her look of thrilling glory is enough to fill his cup forever.

You did it. Good for Hugh.

LAWRENCE HILL has transformed the understanding of many
Canadians, young and old, about this country's history, namely around
the untold legacies of the African slave trade in Canada and the issues
of race and racism that underlie our social fabric. He was born in 1957
in Newmarket, Ontario, to two American immigrants who moved from
Washington, DC, four years earlier. As the son of a black father and a
white mother, both politically active individuals who published their
own work on black history and civil rights issues, much of Hill's work
examines black history and politics. Hill received a bachelor of arts in
economics from Laval University and later earned a master of arts in
creative writing from Johns Hopkins University. He has since been the
recipient of honorary doctorates from several Canadian universities,
including the University of Toronto, the University of Waterloo, Dalhousie
University, and Wilfrid Laurier University. He is also a Senior Fellow at
the University of Toronto's Massey College. Hill worked as a reporter at
the *Globe and Mail* and the *Winnipeg Free Press* and as the Parliamentary
Bureau Chief in Ottawa. As he began his own writing career, Hill was
influenced by the work of his parents; he wrote and curated the Archives
of Ontario exhibit on his father, *The Freedom Seeker: The Life and Times
of Daniel G. Hill* (2006). Hill is the author of several works of nonfiction,

including *Trials and Triumphs: The Story of African-Canadians* (Umbrella Press, 1993), *Women of Vision: The Story of the Canadian Negro Women's Association* (Umbrella Press, 1996), *Black Berry, Sweet Juice: On Being Black and White in Canada* (Flamingo, 2001), *The Deserter's Tale: The Story of an Ordinary Soldier Who Walked Away from the War in Iraq* (House of Anansi Press, 2007) with Joshua Key, the 2012 CLC Kreisel Lecture *Dear Sir, I Intend to Burn Your Book: An Anatomy of a Book Burning* (University of Alberta Press/Canadian Literature Centre, 2013), and the 2013 CBC Massey Lecture *Blood: The Stuff of Life* (House of Anansi Press, 2013).

His article "Is Africa's Pain Black America's Burden?" was published in *The Walrus* and earned him a National Magazine Award. Hill is first and foremost a celebrated fiction writer, with two novels to his name, *Some Great Thing* (Turnstone Press, 1992) and *Any Known Blood* (HarperCollins, 1997), before publishing the award-winning and bestselling novel *The Book of Negroes* (HarperCollins, 2007). Published in some countries as *Someone Knows My Name*, this stunningly successful work won the 2007 Rogers Writers' Trust Fiction Prize and the 2008 Commonwealth Writers' Prize. The novel was also the winner of CBC's Canada Reads competition in 2009, defended by television journalist Avi Lewis, and the winner of Radio-Canada's *Le combat des livres*, where its French translation, *Aminata* (Pleine Lune, 2011), was defended by Québécois musician Thomas Hellman in 2013. The novel has been taken up by a number of reading programs, including those organized by Dalhousie University, Trent University, the Calgary Public Library, the Hamilton Public Library, and the One Book One Community program that links Kitchener, Waterloo, and Cambridge, Ontario. Having sold close to one million copies, *The Book of Negroes* was adapted into a miniseries of the same name (Conquering Lion Pictures, 2015), co-written by Hill and director Clement Virgo. Hill's most recent novel, *The Illegal*, was published by HarperCollins in 2015. He divides his time between his homes in Hamilton, Ontario, and in Woody Point, Newfoundland. Hill visited the Canadian Literature Centre to deliver his Brown Bag Lunch reading on September 11, 2015.

6

LAWRENCE HILL
History and the Truth of Fiction

WINFRIED SIEMERLING

IN BOTH HIS FICTION AND NONFICTION, Lawrence Hill eturns time and again to the experience of race at the intersection of
history and fiction. Mixed race is specifically evident in "Meet You at
the Door," which features Hill's persistent concern with the power of
language and the act of writing itself. The exploration of race in Hill's
fiction has been paralleled by his important documentary contribu-
tions. This work has concentrated in particular on the black experience
in Canada. As the author biography above reveals, Hill has documented
black Canadian history for young readers, written about the Canadian
Negro Women's Association, and scripted a documentary about the
black church in Canada. A former reporter for the *Globe and Mail* and
the *Winnipeg Free Press*, he continues to write for newspapers and mag-
azines, and his 2013 Massey lectures about the social constructions of
biological categories, *Blood: The Stuff of Life*, have underlined his role as a
public intellectual.

Hill first wrote fiction full-time during a year in Spain in 1985, after
studying economics at francophone Laval University in Québec, a visit
to Africa in 1979, and five years as a newspaper reporter. His newspaper
experience is fictionalized in his first novel, *Some Great Thing* (1992). The
narrator is a black reporter returning to his native Winnipeg, where
poverty, race, and French–English linguistic conflict in Manitoba feature

prominently in his articles. He also re-enters a difficult relationship with his father, a former railroad porter who extols the virtues of race consciousness and black history. Together with the stories and documents accumulated on the job, the father's boxes with black history clippings and family documents soon enter the imagination of the initially reluctant narrator and begin to change his life. *Some Great Thing* is a Bildungsroman whose narrator, a researcher and witness, comes to understand himself by writing about the lives of others and the past. Stylistically, the novel enlists the powers of humour and gentle satire to engage the reader. A Cameroonian journalist, for instance, provides counterpoint and seemingly innocent social comment, reporting from an African perspective on his often puzzling Canadian experience in Winnipeg. He will return in Hill's second novel and again in his most recent one, *The Illegal* (2015).

Any Known Blood (1997) develops some of these formal and thematic aspects. The narrator of this overtly metafictional novel is a fiction writer whose dual search for identity and black history is articulated in the work we read. Like Hill's subsequent memoir, *Black Berry, Sweet Juice: On Being Black and White in Canada* (2001), *Any Known Blood* announces its concern with mixed race in the title. The protagonist's name, Langston Cane V, further signals Harlem Renaissance comment on mixed race by Langston Hughes and the author of *Cane*, Jean Toomer. The novel follows the narrator's journey in search of family and black history across five generations and on both sides of the Canada–US border. Exploring racial passing, ascription, and identification, the novel shows the narrator's journey from ambivalence and isolation to an understanding of the past, the importance of community, and the ability to act in the present.

For readers of Hill's art, it is fascinating to observe how the protagonist's quest for identity occurs in conversation with black North American history and writing. It culminates in his encounter with a forebear's slave narrative. With this substantial neo-slave narrative, which constitutes the second-last chapter, Hill draws inspiration from the first literary form of black testimony. One of its foremost practitioners, Frederick Douglass makes a brief appearance in the novel, which also uses some passages from his writings (identified in "A Note about History" at the end). Other important textual antecedents include black Canadian narratives such as those collected by Benjamin Drew in *The Refugee: The Narratives of Fugitive Slaves in Canada* (1856) or Osborne P. Anderson's *A Voice from Harper's Ferry* (1861), the only participant account of John Brown's 1859 ill-fated raid on the US federal armory. In the notes at the end of the book, we further learn about Hill's interviews with his father and a local historian, which supplement these written sources with oral history.

Hill merges history with fiction again in *The Book of Negroes* (2007). The very title invokes a textual antecedent, the 1783 military ledger commonly known as Guy Carleton's Book of Negroes. The title word "Negroes" initially caused Hill's US publisher to issue the novel as *Someone Knows My Name*, while some Dutch descendants of Surinam slaves even burned a photocopy of the title page in public. In an article in *The Guardian* and in his CLC Kreisel Lecture, *Dear Sir, I Intend to Burn Your Book*, Hill responded by thoughtfully contextualizing the title with regard to history and changing racial designations. As he points out in the lecture, "the entire point of the novel [is] to offer dignity, depth, and dimensionality to a person whose humanity would have been assaulted as a slave" (6). Hill formally underlines this claim by writing the novel entirely as a neo-slave narrative. He adopts the conventions of original slave narratives (such as descriptions of cruelty, captivity, and personal experience) and tells the story through the memorably strong voice of a protagonist who remembers slavery and freedom in her old age. Hill's narrator, Aminata, is abducted as a young girl in Africa, survives the middle passage, and suffers slavery in South Carolina. She escapes to serve the British during the American Revolutionary War and in 1783 flees with other Loyalists from New York to Shelburne, Nova Scotia. Disappointed with the conditions she encounters there, she joins the exodus of other black Nova Scotians to Sierra Leone in 1792, and ends her life in London.

While Hill's epic black Atlantic narrative unfolds the trauma of slavery, displacement, and post-slavery racism and struggle, it is also crucially concerned with the power of language, witness, and writing.

Aminata speaks Bamanankan and Fulfulde, learns to write a few Arabic phrases as a child, and then adds English in a range of registers. She also becomes a voracious reader—of newspapers, Swift, Voltaire, and Olaudah Equiano's famous slave narrative—and, most importantly, acquires the vital skill of writing. Throughout the novel, we see her using her multilingual talents to channel information and create community, employing language tactically to intervene in realities otherwise beyond her control. Her ultimate goal is to become a *djeli*, or storyteller, and bear witness. A similar attitude to language and writing is apparent in Hill's own transformative approach to history and the past. Most crucially, he makes his protagonist—a woman and a former slave—not only the narrator of his novel but also a scribe of the 1783 Book of Negroes, the military register naming three thousand black individuals who were allowed to sail mostly to Nova Scotia before the British surrender New York. Hill shows the potentially transformative force of writing when Aminata adds small details and context to the terse ledger entries she is asked to record, supplementing the documentary historiography of the British Empire. The stakes of inscription are revealed again when Aminata writes her own story at the end of her life, and the British abolitionists around William Wilberforce offer to relieve her of the task. Having his inkpot-wielding narrator insist on her own version, however, Hill highlights the neo-slave narrative's task of imagining what white editorial control and the politics of the slave narrative have historically relegated to silence.

In London, Aminata herself thus writes back to the Empire that once helped to enslave her, coming to haunt it at its very centre. Structurally, the novel moves back and forth between the scene of writing in London and the account of her life, unfolding the act of witnessing in temporal dimensions that include the moment of experience and the later one of giving testimony. A future dimension is invoked when Aminata muses about the effect of her written narrative on future audiences, ethically implicating the readers of Hill's novel. With Aminata's life trajectory and self-conception as a storyteller whose testimony relates the past to the future, Hill configures a diasporic subject beyond the trope of return. His protagonist comes to London after realizing that her dream of returning home has become impossible. Aminata reflects on the past but now finds identity and meaning in the transformative power that witnessing has in the present, and in the community to come that it makes possible in the future.

As noted earlier, *The Book of Negroes* has been highly successful in alerting contemporary audiences to black history and lives in a diaspora that includes what is now Canada. Giving what Hill calls "dignity, depth, and dimensionality" (*Dear Sir* 6) to victims and survivors of slavery, the novel fleshes out and humanizes black diasporic lives rendered mostly invisible by our dominant modes of knowledge. Similar narrative goals mark a recent and a forthcoming novel by Hill. *The Illegal* portrays a refugee from Africa who is forced to navigate life in a rich country without the comforts and security of legal recognition and citizenship. A subsequent novel will revisit the contribution of black soldiers to the building of the Alaska Highway during the Second World War.

Hill's short stories have appeared in magazines and anthologies but remain unpublished in book form. Several of them are based on his travel experiences; his first published story, "My Side of the Fence" (*Descant*, 1980), and "Perpetual and Everlasting" (*West Coast Line*, 1995) are set in Africa, while "El Negrito" (*Blood and Aphorisms*, 1991) and "Concepción" (*Exile*, 1988) take place in Spain. Like the one excerpted here, "Meet You at the Door," stories by Hill can be usefully juxtaposed with the novels. "Concepción" features a female narrator who is a reporter, while the narrator of "Victim Stories" (*Blood and Aphorisms*, 1991) has much in common with the reporter in *Some Great Thing*. Many of the stories also evoke the theme of mixed race. In "My Side of the Fence," a narrator of mixed descent faces his own racial insecurities while travelling in Africa. A Romany character experiences overt racism in "El Negrito," but his skin colour often also causes the seemingly innocent question endured by the narrators of *Some Great Thing* and *Any Known Blood*: "Where are you from?" A young girl from Don Mills, Ontario (where Hill himself grew up), is interrogated more blatantly in "So What Are You, Anyway?" (published in Ayanna Black's *Fiery Spirits and Voices*).

Like that story, "Meet You at the Door" is set in 1970s Canada, although the temporal distancing of the opening phrase—"This happened in the dinosaur days"—might subtly mock our current multicultural complacencies about race relations in this country. Spatially, the story tells us that race is a Canadian subject, right here at home. And as with so much of Hill's fiction, the writer-narrator nimbly handles language and connects voices and events across time and space, while registering the impact of a haunting past. Communication is ubiquitously evoked through its materiality—the L.C. Smith, railways, foot pedals, hoops, microphones, and radio—but also takes place through voices in the head. A worthy student of his teacher "Tolstoy," who keeps "an entire network of moving trains in his head" (Hill, "Meet You" 63), the writer-narrator is a fast-typing operator. He orchestrates voices and steers communication as words and trains of thought come barrelling down on him with great speed, some with dangerous hazards attached to them.

Hill's work tells us much about history and is extensive in its temporal and geographical reach from eighteenth-century Africa right down to the here and now of a Canada we thought we knew. The marvelous effect of his writing is to make readers realize that events relate to each other across distances of time and space. His narrators show us how they—and we—can realize those connections that often have to be concretized through the personal and necessary truth of the imagination.

Works Cited

Anderson, Osborne Perry. *A Voice from Harper's Ferry.* Boston: Printed for the author, 1861. Print.

Drew, Benjamin. 1856. *The Refugee; or The Narratives of Fugitive Slaves in Canada. Related By Themselves, with An Account of the History and Condition of the Colored Population of Upper Canada.* Toronto: Prospero, 2000. Print.

Hill, Lawrence. *Any Known Blood.* Toronto: HarperCollins, 1997. Print.

——. *Blood: The Stuff of Life.* CBC Massey Lectures Series. Toronto: House of Anansi Press, 2013. Print.

——. *The Book of Negroes.* Toronto: HarperCollins, 2007. Print.

———. "Concepción." *Exile* 13.1 (1998): 18-44. Print.

———. *Dear Sir, I Intend to Burn Your Book: An Anatomy of a Book Burning.* Edmonton: University of Alberta Press/Canadian Literature Centre, 2013. Print.

———. *The Illegal.* Toronto: HarperCollins, 2015. Print.

———. "Meet You at the Door." *The Walrus* 8.1 (2011): 60-67. Print.

———. "My Side of the Fence." *Descant* 11.4 (1980): 69-78. Print.

———. "El Negrito." *Blood and Aphorisms* 2 (1991): 20-25. Print.

———. "Perpetual and Everlasting." *West Coast Line 16* 29.1 (1995): 91-94. Print.

———. "So What Are You, Anyway?" *Fiery Spirit and Voices.* Ed. Ayanna Black. Toronto: HarperCollins, 2000. 251-56. Print.

———. *Some Great Thing.* Winnipeg: Turnstone Press, 1992. Print.

———. "Victim Stories." *Blood and Aphorisms* 3 (1991): 17-20. Print.

Meet You at the Door (excerpt)

THIS HAPPENED back in the dinosaur days, in the town of Gull Lake, Saskatchewan, population 800. The gulls had all died, and the lake had dried up. On the Saskatchewan farmlands, oil pumps bobbed up and down, looking like black grasshoppers on steroids. Folks were fuming about the metric system and had a nickname for the new top-loading railway car: a Trudeau hopper. I had other preoccupations. A ghost had chased me out of university and had hounded me for a year in Greece, Italy, France, and Spain. And now I was back in Canada, to take a summer job in a place where I knew no one.

I had hitchhiked into town to work in the one-room station of the Canadian Pacific Railway. On my left arm, balanced against my chest, was an L.C. Smith typewriter, heavy enough to be a weapon of war. Catapulted over a battlefield, it could have taken a man out. In my right hand was a classical guitar, purchased in Granada from the man who made it. On my back was a knapsack, stitched with the Canadian flag, so Europeans wouldn't take me for an American. It was 1977. The summer job was part of my recovery plan.

I walked past The Mad Dog bar and into town, ringing doorbells and asking to rent a room. On my sixth attempt, a woman answered. She looked like she had been born around the time of my great-grandmother. Everything about her was white. Hair. Socks. Nursing shoes. On her clothesline out back, flapping in the wind, hung white underwear the size of a parachute. She stood no taller than five feet. Blue eyes, clear as lake water. She stepped back when she saw me, but listened as I spoke. She said she wouldn't mind my working nights. She said her own son Jimmy could keep a job for about as long as she could hold a spooked horse.

She said I was welcome to stay for twenty-five dollars a month. Her name was Eleanor Hadfield. She had been widowed long ago. As she spoke, Mrs. Hadfield kept checking out my hair.

Have you ever seen a mammoth pine tree in southern Spain? No branches all the way up, but at the top there is an eruption of foliage. I had an Afro like that. Also, I was dark. Like the best part of a chocolate éclair. Some of my looks came from my father and his people. And some came from spending much of the past year in southern Europe. I had stayed in shared rooms, youth hostel style, sleeping inches from strangers, one looking clubbed and comatose, and the next snoring like a purring brontosaurus. I had changed cities every night, on the run from that voice in my head.

Come on, it said. *It's not so bad. Can you provide me with one good reason to go on living? Come over this way,* it said, *I'll meet you at the door.* For a year, the voice had been tracking me like a bounty hunter.

From my bedroom one Sunday morning, I heard Mrs. Hadfield's son railing about me. In the small house, I heard every word. Why had she not consulted him before renting to me? What if I ransacked her house? Have you considered this, her son kept saying, have you even looked at him? Jimmy, she said, he's a gentleman—may not look like one, but he is. Mother, he said, nothing good can come of this. Jimmy, she said, eat your pie.

Soon enough, Eleanor Hadfield began to ask me to join her in the kitchen for pies, cakes, cookies, and roast beef. Most of all, she liked serving me potatoes. Fried, baked, cookie-thin and roasted, or boiled. Under gravy, over rice, in casseroles, or all alone.

One day while I was writing, she brought me a mug of tea and said, "I got more ways for potato than all the keys on your typewriter."

"I bet you do."

She ran her finger along the platen of my L.C. Smith and declared that it was as smooth and hard as her rolling pin. "What are you so busy writing?"

"Just trying to get my thoughts out."

"I hear you typing half the day," she said. "Fingers coming down like rain."

"Does the sound bother you?"

"No," she said. "It's the sound of you being here."

| Passenger trains didn't stop in Gull Lake, but freight trains had to pull off onto the side tracks to let other trains overtake or pass them on the single track across the prairie. The dispatcher in Calgary and conductors moving all across Saskatchewan and Alberta could not communicate directly. They had to go through me—the operator. I took orders from the dispatcher and passed them along to the trains highballing east and west through town.

I worked alone in the station, starting at 7 p.m. and often working until 6 a.m. It was up to me to know more than any person in the world about the trains that thundered each night through Gull Lake, Saskatchewan. I had to radio for permission to leave the chair and go to the bathroom. I radioed again, once back in the chair. The dispatcher in Calgary knew how often I pissed in an eleven-hour shift, and how long it took me. It was a firing offense to fall asleep at the desk.

My job was to type up the dispatcher's orders and to pass them along to oncoming trains. I had to be able to type them up at fifty words a minute. Typos were not allowed. It was in the rule book: if you made a typo, you had to say so. Then you had to rip up your order and ask the dispatcher to give it to you all over again, while you typed. While the train was bearing down on you at fifty miles an hour.

I had two radios to manage. On my left, the one for incoming and outbound trains. It only worked when a train was within a five-mile radius. This radio connected me to the conductor in the caboose. It was the conductor who did all the talking—to me and, through me, to the dispatcher. In the radio to my right, I could hear the dispatcher any time, but he could only hear me when I pushed a foot pedal under my desk.

One Tuesday in June, weeks after I had settled into the job, a conductor got in my ear at 2:49 a.m. He was on a westbound train. Number 901. I knew it. It was a freight train. Usually about 100 cars. More than a mile long. Travelling at full speed, a beast like that took ten minutes to stop.

"Gullick. You there?" It was the voice of an old man. Some conductors liked to kid around on the radio. Others were all business. This one sounded as if he liked to hunt bears, drink beer, and watch strippers.

I pulled the train mike closer. "Gull Lake here."

"Are they robbing the cradle?" he said. "What are you, sixteen?"

You kept your mouth shut with the dispatcher, but conductors were fair game. So I said, "And are they stealing from graves these days? No live bodies left?"

His guffaw sounded like a machine gun. "Looky-looky, we have one with attitude. Heaven help us. What are you, a student?"

"Sort of."

"*Sort of.* We got a politician in Gullick. We got a right regular Pierre Trudeau." He pronounced the prime minister's name "*pee*-air." He chuckled into the radio.

I pictured him being sixty years old, which, at three times my age, seemed ancient. About five-seven. One hundred and ninety, with a pot belly and stick-thin legs. "So," he added, "got anything for me?"

He was testing me, trying to see if I would do him a favour and break the rules. He knew that operators were not allowed to reveal the dispatcher's orders over the radio. "Should know soon," I said. "Where are you?"

"Five point one miles out."

"Stand by," I said.

I didn't know who was dispatching that night. The dispatcher would have started his shift minutes earlier. He would be feeling his way into the night, and calling me any moment. Each night presented a puzzle, needing a unique solution.

Each night, the dispatcher in Calgary had to draw a map of the prairies, and send dozens of trains through it. Quickly. Safely. Fast trains had priority over slow ones. Passenger trains had priority over some freight trains but not others. It was complicated. And that was when no animals wandered onto the tracks. A train could throw a deer or a bear as easily as a boy could pitch a baseball. But a sow was heavy and thick and had a low centre of gravity. She was the mammal most likely to derail a train.

"Gull Lake," the dispatcher called, "you there?"

I kept my answer short and simple: "Gull Lake."

He let a long, slow laugh percolate down the railway line. But I knew, before the laugh, who he was. Just about every dispatcher, conductor, and operator working for the Canadian Pacific Railway in the age of the dinosaur pronounced the town "Gullick." So I knew, after just two words, who occupied the dispatcher's chair. His name was Weedman, but privately I had nicknamed him Tolstoy. He pronounced the town the way it was written. Pronounced it the same way I said it: "Gull Lake." Pausing for a nanosecond between each word.

Tolstoy had been the lead instructor in my two-week train operators' course in Calgary. He didn't speak much to me during the course, but took a good, long look at me on the first day. Before the day ended, he said, "Where are you from, man?" He didn't use "man" with anybody else in the course. But nobody else in the course looked like me. I told him Toronto and left it at that.

| "Hello, white boy," Tolstoy said to me through the radio.

Tolstoy had never called me "white boy" during training, never to my face. For that, he waited until he had me on the line, where other operators would hear our conversation. He waited to trot out "white boy" until I had a train bearing down on me. I didn't care what he called me. I had known worse.

On Christmas Day of my second year at university, my best friend's mother called and begged me to come over. I sat so worried about their pain that I didn't know how to touch my own. They poured endless mugs of tea, in the hope that I could tell them something about their son—chess player, world traveller, hobby Marxist and book klepto. In my dreams, I became accountable for everything Howie had stolen. Even his own life. It was my responsibility to explain it, to make up for it. In my dreams, he would accuse me of living a phony life. I would reply that he had given up too soon. Come over here, he said, and I'll prove it. Come this way. *I'll meet you at the door.*

"Any word from 901?" Tolstoy said.

I glanced at my watch. "One minute ago, he was five miles east of Gull Lake." That meant I had four minutes to take down Tolstoy's order, arrange the original and the carbon copy, clip one each onto wooden hoops, and get myself out the door and onto the platform.

"Where'd you learn to type so fast?" Tolstoy asked.

"My mother taught me on her L.C. Smith."

"That takes the cake. White boy's mother taught him to type? Who *does* that?"

I let the silence build. Maybe Tolstoy would take the hint.

"So, is your mom white?"

"Beg your pardon?"

"Well, you're mixed, right? I'm figuring you didn't get the hair from your mom."

"Why not?" I asked.

"Didn't you say that she taught you to type?"

"What are you saying, Tolstoy?"

He paused. Coughed. And then pulled rank. "What did you just call me?"

It was ridiculous, this rule of having to take all manner of trash talk from the dispatcher but not being allowed to talk back.

"Tolstoy was a fine writer," I said. "But don't take *War and Peace* to work—you might fall asleep on the job."

He laughed. "You have some nerve." He let a moment pass, and then asked: "Is Johnson conducting the 901?"

"I'll find out."

I pushed away the dispatcher's mike and pulled the conductor's radio closer.

"Dispatcher wants to know if it's Johnson conducting."

"Yep. And let me guess who's in the chair in Calgary," the conductor said. "It's Weedman, right?"

"Yup," I said. But I never thought of the dispatcher as Weedman, even though it worked with his goatee. If Tolstoy had any sense, he would go back to school before he flamed out. They said five years was the longest any dispatcher had lasted. Nervous breakdowns. Ulcers. What thinking person would take a job that was known to drive delicate souls to suicide?

The dispatcher radioed me again. "Gull Lake, are you ready?"

I rolled the order paper with the carbon copy into the typewriter. "Ready."

Tolstoy fired off a message I had learned to decode and type, at top speed and with no mistakes, in training. He said it once. I heard it and kept listening while blasting away on the typewriter keys so the carbon copy would look clear. In a nutshell, this is what he told me:

"Westbound 901, take siding no. 2 at Maple Creek July 23 at three hours aught aught minutes and allow Westbound no. 463 to pass at three hours aught eight minutes. At three hours twelve minutes, continue westbound, maximum thirty miles per hour, direction Calgary. Prepare for more orders at Medicine Hat."

I finished a breath after his last word and read it back to him. There was a mistake in the word "Medicine." I had typed it "Mecicine." But now it was too late. I had no time to start all over again. I banked on the theory that the engineer and the conductor wouldn't notice it or report it, so I told Tolstoy that the sheet was clean and I had made no mistakes.

"You're good, Williams."

So. The dispatcher had dropped "white boy," and was back to using my name again.

Thirty seconds later, the conductor buzzed me on the radio. "Gullick, whaddya got for me?"

If I revealed the orders and the dispatcher got wind of it, I would be sacked for violating rule no. 21, which Tolstoy had summarized in training as *Don't tell the conductor a single thing on the radio, because if he gets it wrong you could be looking at two things: a train derailment and lifelong unemployment.* But if I didn't give the conductor something, he might report my typo. So I said, "Prepare for a long order." Then I pressed down the foot pedal to the dispatcher, so he could hear the conductor hollering at me through his radio.

"Tell that college dropout dispatcher I'm going rip his head off and pitch it to the seagulls," the conductor said.

"901, where are you now?" I said, still with my foot down for the dispatcher's benefit.

"Two point four miles east of you," the conductor said.

Tolstoy laughed for the benefit of all the operators listening in on our conversation. "Tell him to fire up his coffee pot," Tolstoy said.

Turning my mouth to the connection to the conductor, I said, "The dispatcher says to enjoy the coffee in Maple Creek."

"There is no coffee in Maple Creek," the conductor said. "Tell that goateed golden boy—" He kept ranting while I prepared the hoops. I asked permission to leave my desk to go hoop up the train.

"Yes, Williams," the dispatcher said. "Stand steady against the wind. And watch out. Reports of a Trudeau hopper with a loose wire. Stay back, but try to give me the exact location of that hopper."

I ran outside with the two hoops that allowed, in the age of dinosaurs, for formal communication between the train and the dispatcher. Each hoop was shaped like a number nine.

A loop and a long neck. The big one had a loop about eighteen inches in diameter and a neck about four feet long. The short one had the same loop, but a neck of just a foot or so.

At the intersection of the loop and the neck was a metal clip. Into the clip of each hoop, I attached the message from Tolstoy in Calgary. Using the hoops, I would have to pass up the fresh copy of the train order to the engineer leaning out the front car of the train. Then I would have to step back and wait for the train to thunder by, stepping back up to the edge of the platform in time to hoop up the conductor in the caboose at the back of the train.

Outside, the sky was lit with stars, and the wind pushed hard from the west. I stood by the edge of the track and saw the train's headlight, like a burning star itself, growing brighter. The train whistle wailed like a broken man. Distorted, dopplerized, it came at me like a parent, mightily aggrieved and forever offended. The rails shook by my feet.

| After Howie hanged himself from the branch of a tree in High Park, his mother glued herself to me, desperate for explanations I couldn't offer. But Howie also stuck to me. He didn't care where I slept, or how much I paid for a cot in a youth hostel.

The dead had an unfair advantage. They could hector you all they wanted through the deepest, darkest Saskatchewan nights, where there was no movement but oil pumps bobbing in agreement. When the dead spoke, it was always a monologue.

| I held my ground against the rumbling rails and the judgmental train wail and the wind that swirled under the belly of the train. As the locomotive drew near, I hoisted the long hoop high some twelve feet overhead, angling it toward the path of the train so the circle in the number nine became a hole through which the engineer could punch his arm. The train barrelled forward. I saw the engineer lean out the window, bending his arm into the shape of an L. I released the hoop at the instant the engineer put his fist through the hoop, caught it, and lifted it up and away from me. He plucked out my message and threw down the hoop.

I stepped back to avoid the swirling wire, wherever it was. I counted back from the lead locomotive. Car one. Car two. Car three. Starting at car eighteen, a string of Trudeau hoppers. They irritated some farmers, because you could only load grain in them, and only from the top.

Car twenty-five was a black Trudeau hopper, dragging a loose wire and intent on laceration. I danced back and jumped. The wire swirled and hissed underneath me. I thought of my mother, and how she would have freaked out if she knew I was being paid seven dollars an hour to dance out of reach of slashing wires. And I thought of Eleanor Hadfield, sleeping in the night. The day before, she had come down to my room, sat down on my bed, and placed her hand on my shoulder. I jumped as if I'd been shocked by the paddles of a defibrillator. I opened my eyes. She invited me upstairs. It was one in the afternoon, she said, and I had been screaming. Something about my shoe caught in the railway tracks with a train coming on. Come upstairs, she said, for potato with more character than the prime minister of Canada. I followed her, and slid into a chair at her table. The potatoes were steaming and ready, on a china plate. Eleanor Hadfield had tugged them straight from her garden. They were scrubbed, halved, and boiled to perfection: just a hint of resistance against the tines of my fork.

I smothered them in butter and fresh parsley, salted them to taste, took the first bite, and thought, *I have never eaten a potato before.*

| The train stretched more than a mile long. It had slowed to thirty miles an hour. I got ready, stepping closer. I could see the last Trudeau hopper, and then the caboose. The conductor was leaning out, taking a good look at me. I was all lit up on the station platform. He was calculating the height at which I held the hoop. He was 200 yards away. One hundred. Fifty. Johnson was closer to the ground than the engineer, and easier to hoop up. No need to reach high in the wind. The conductor was up just a foot above me, so it was practically an intimate encounter. As he bore down on me and stuck out his arm for the catch, I heard him call out, "By Christ, it's a nigger." And then his mouth fell. He knew I had heard him.

Johnson caught the hoop. The wind blew his hat off. The 901 drew away, and I hunted for the two hoops among the grass and stones. I also found the conductor's cap. I made my way back to the station and told Tolstoy in Calgary that I had hooped up both ends of the train, and that the loose wire was twenty-five cars back from the locomotive. But I did not tell Tolstoy that the conductor had radioed me, from his position a mile west of Gull Lake, while he was still inside radio radius.

"Gullick," the conductor said, "what's your name, anyways?"

"Williams."

"Got a first name?"

"Joel."

"Well, Joel, don't mind an ignorant old man, and don't take offence. I'm not prejudiced. I just never saw the likes of you before in Gullick. You hoop up like a pro. Don't be mad."

"No sweat," I told Johnson. It all came down to dignity. And the easiest way to retain my dignity was to act like it didn't mean a thing.

"You've got a loose wire twenty-five cars back from the front," I told Johnson.

"Did it hit you? You okay?"

"It's swirling around. But I'm okay."

"I'll check it out at Maple Creek," he said, pronouncing it "Crick." And then he continued, "After all, we don't want to be taking out our college students, irregardless of race."

I didn't call him on the word "irregardless." I just said, "I found your cap."

"Hang onto it for me. And son, I won't tell Weedman about how you spell 'Medicine.'"

"Thanks," I said.

"You a university kid?" he asked.

"Yup," I said.

"Where you going?"

"The University of British Columbia," I told him, "if I make it back there."

"Damn right you'll make it back there. Are your parents proud?"

I didn't want to tell him I had lost my father months before my best friend went and ruined Christmas Day. So I just said that my mom wanted to see me back in school.

"Good call," he said. "Train jobs are going the way of the dodo bird. I'll make a deal with you. In September, on one of my overnights in Vancouver, I'll come out to U B C and make sure you started up again."

"It's way out on a peninsula. Point Grey."

"Son, I know every city in Canada that has a train station in it. I get a day or two off, and I go walking. What's the name of the building you study in, out there at U B C on Point Grey?"

"Buchanan."

"Name is Johnson," he said. "Ed Johnson. Look for me at Buchanan. I'll bring you a back-to-school gift, high noon on the first Saturday after Labour Day, and I'll meet you at the door."

There was some kind of gravel in his voice that felt good to hear. He sounded like an old fart of a grandfather in that moment. Something in his voice made me feel I'd soon be getting through the nights again. Dream-free.

ALICE MAJOR is a prolific writer with over a dozen books to her name. She has been writing for over two decades and has received a number of awards and honours for her work. Major was born in Scotland and spent her early life in Dumbarton, and immigrated to Canada at the age of eight. She grew up in Toronto, Ontario, later moving to central British Columbia to take a job as a newspaper reporter for the *Williams Lake Tribune*. In 1981, Major moved to Edmonton, Alberta, where she continues to reside. Her first book, *The Chinese Mirror* (Clarke Irwin, 1988), was a finalist for the Canadian Library Association Book of the Year in 1988, as well as the winner of the Alberta Writing for Youth Competition. She then published *Time Travels Light* (Rowan, 1992), and two chapbooks, *Complete with Herself* (Hawthorne Society, 1997) and *Scenes from the Sugar Bowl Café* (BS Poetry Society, 1998), which won the Shaunt Basmajian Chapbook Competition. She then published *Lattice of the Years* (Bayeux Arts, 1999), which was shortlisted for the City of Edmonton Book Prize, followed by *Tales for an Urban Sky* (Broken Jaw Press, 1999), for which she was awarded the Poets' Corner Award and shortlisted for the Stephan G. Stephansson Award and the City of Edmonton Book Prize. Next, Major published *Corona Radiata* (St. Thomas Press, 2000), *No Monster* (Poppy Press, 2001), and *Some Bones and a Story* (Wolsak and Wynn, 2001), which was shortlisted for the Pat Lowther Memorial Award. Major followed these books with *The Occupied World* (University of Alberta Press, 2006), which was shortlisted for the Stephan G. Stephansson Award, and *The Office Tower Tales* (University of Alberta Press, 2008), which was awarded the Book Publishers Association of Alberta's Trade Book of the Year (fiction), won the Pat Lowther Memorial Award, and was shortlisted for the City of Edmonton Book Prize. Shortly after, she published *Memory's Daughter* (University of Alberta Press, 2010) and *Intersecting Sets: A Poet Looks at Science* (University of Alberta Press, 2011), which won the Wilfrid Eggleston Award and a 2012 National Magazine Award Gold Medal for "The Ultraviolent Catastrophe," an essay that formed part of *Intersecting Sets*. Major then published a young adult fantasy e-book, *The Jade Spindle* (eSisters, 2012). Her most recent book of poetry, *Standard candles* (University of Alberta Press, 2015), was shortlisted for the Raymond Souster Award and the Stephan G. Stephansson Award. Major's poetry has appeared in such periodicals as *Antigonish Review, Arc, CV2, Descant, Grain Magazine, Literary Review of Canada, The Malahat Review, The New Quarterly, PRISM International*, and *Queen's Quarterly*. Her work has also been widely anthologized, in *On Spec: The First Five Years* (Tesseract Books, 1995), *Threshold: An Anthology of Contemporary Writing from Alberta* (University of Alberta Press, 2000), *Writing the City: Poets Laureate of Edmonton* (Edmonton Arts Council, 2012), and *Untying the Apron: Daughters Remember Mothers of the 1950s* (Guernica Editions, 2013). Major is a member of the League of Canadian Poets, the Writers' Guild of Alberta, the Edmonton Arts Council, and served as Edmonton's first poet laureate. In 2012, Major was awarded the Queen Elizabeth II Diamond Jubilee Medal. Alice Major visited the Canadian Literature Centre to deliver a Brown Bag Lunch reading on March 19, 2008, and again on March 13, 2013.

7

ALICE MAJOR
Metaphors, Myths, and the Eye of the Magpie

ALICE MAJOR IS BEST KNOWN as an award-winning poet. Yet over her distinguished and multifaceted career, she has also produced an enviable body of essays, articles, and lectures that extend beyond literature into the fields of science and mathematics—two of her lifelong passions. Critically important is her award-winning set of essays *Intersecting Sets: A Poet Looks at Science.* Like her lecture "A Superposition of Brains," the essays reflect her understanding of how the human mind works and makes valuable connections between the creative and imaginative aspects shared by the supposedly separate worlds of "emotional" art and "rational" science. Together with other comments found in prefaces to collections of her poetry, the essays and lecture help readers appreciate the purpose, range, and vitality of Major's own fountain of observations, measurements, myth, and history. These are the material foundation and often the subject matter of her poetry, as in "The Office Romeo's Tale," discussed further below.

By her own frequent self-defining metaphor, to read the world through the words and vision of Alice Major is to read it through the eyes and scavenging impulses of a "magpie." Major explains in "The Magpie's Eye," the introduction to *Intersecting Sets*, how she has been forever "picking up bright, oddly-shaped ideas that attracted me from various disciplines and arranging them along with anecdotes that I hope give them context" (xvi). These ideas, or as she calls them in the Preface to *Tales for an Urban Sky*, these "glittery things" (7), are the raw material she builds into "some home structure" (7), her poetry and other writing. The home structures become new glittery objects in their own right for other magpie eyes, those of her readers, to fasten onto and to organize into home structures of their own, and form a network of linked understanding.

Major's references to the magpie and the home structure are, of course, metaphors, which, along with related rhetorical structures and literary figures, are at the heart not only of her writing, but her understanding of how the human mind makes sense of the world. As she explains in the unpublished lecture "A Superposition of Brains," as "pattern recognizing, pattern-making animals," humans "[think] metaphorically all the time." Through induction, observation, and "our amazing ability for statistical analysis," which allow us to detect regular and unusual patterns in life and language, we are always making connections, realizing analogies, and getting that "little kick of satisfaction that says 'You've correctly figured out a pattern. You've recognized something.'"

Major's definition of metaphor, however, is more complex and playful than the standard correct answer on a school quiz. Metaphorical connections, says Major in her essay "Metaphor at Play," rest on the human "ability to hold two situations in mind at once,... and to fool around with the combo" (18). Those two situations, as she explains further in "A Superposition of Brains," compare and link the "here" (what a literary critic might call the tenor, or the thing itself) with the "not here" (the vehicle used to explain it by comparative association). The range and variety of Major's connected "heres" and "not heres" are at once definitively personal and yet never so private as to be inaccessible.

A few examples suggest the fuller scope. *Tales for an Urban Sky* engages in the human capacity for myth making, which Major sees as a local activity as compared to the larger body of mythologies that are continuous across time. The poems in the title section frame the local against the phases of the moon, as patterned and named after everyday

urban items familiar in what has become her home, Edmonton, "a
northern Alberta city that is like and unlike any other place" (7). The
glittery objects include such items as lost grocery carts, tall glass build-
ings, parked cars, and (of course) quarrelling magpies. Each "Moon"
so named is accompanied by a verse fable, fairy tale, or folk myth to
flesh out the image. A second section identifies places around the city
against the figures and functions of Mayan number gods. Major devel-
oped an interest in Mayan culture and history over trips to Mexico, and
traces of her subsequent research appear elsewhere in her writing as
well, including "The Office Romeo's Tale" reproduced here. A third sec-
tion of *Tales for an Urban Sky* builds on scenes observed in coffee shops
or from coffee shop windows.

The Occupied World begins with a series called "Contemplating
the City," which links places and events from Edmonton against
ceremonies and injunctions practiced to establish a colony of Rome,
again expanding on the theme and work of building home structures.

Memory's Daughter, which rests on family history and connections,
contains a section named "Metamorphoses." The poems trace the
physically debilitating effects of a degenerative condition on a young
woman, contrasted with her bright spirit and determination. They
capture and forge parallels with transformations narrated in Ovid's
well-known collection of tales that detail the sometimes helpful,
sometimes painful changes worked on people through contact with
the gods or divine intervention in human affairs. A second section
called "The Great Work" traces the path of a marriage and family
through a series of ghazals (an ancient Middle Eastern form that
typically took love as a theme) named for the stages of alchemical
processes that sought to "marry" Sun and Moon to attempt to create
the ideal, the Philosopher's Stone.

This small sample suggests the rich range of experience and
curiosity feeding and supporting the pattering mind behind Major's
magpie vision, and the potential for enjoyment and education to be
found in her poetry. Metaphors and other related figures, Major affirms,
are after all not just decorations, any more than are the emphatic
arrangements of sounds that draw poetic attention to a line and an

image. They are means of building the home structure that is the poet's means of communication, not just as a poet but as a human seeking communication with other humans.

Once Major feels that kick of emotion at recognizing a connection or intuiting a pattern, her next task is to celebrate it and give it expressive, communicative shape and voice through what she has termed "linguistic virtuosity" ("The Poetry Fan" 14), the poetic techniques of repetition, rhyme, rhythm, and metre that help emphasize what matters in the connection. Consider two examples:

> The whole planet a small, throbbing,
>   blinking jukebox floating around the sun ("Messages From Planet E")

and

> the thrumming calculus of life comes
> to completion ("Zeno's Paradox")

These vivid metaphors—planet = jukebox or machine for playing back music; life = calculus, or mathematical calculation—are also examples of onomatopoeia. Also at work are repeated vowel and consonant sounds and regular patterns of stressed and unstressed syllables, occasionally interrupted by other sounds and stresses that at key moments become calculated poetic stop signs (as Major has termed them) to make a reader pause briefly to consider and appreciate some little glittering something along the way. All such combined techniques of figurative language and sound create words that clearly connect poet and audience through "images that will lead a reader or listener to say, 'Yes, that's apt, that's right; that clicks for me, too, as a description of the world'" ("Metaphor at Play" 43). The shared clicks help create what Major calls in her essay "That Frost Feeling" a "community of communicants" (9). The essay itself is about the ways humans create such communities from "opportunities to experience the sensations of empathy" (9) that are created by shared chances to "respond to artifacts, sounds, stories, images" (9).

A community of communicants is at the heart of Major's extended verse narrative *The Office Tower Tales*, from which "The Office Romeo's Tale" is excerpted. *The Office Tower Tales* display the wide scope of Major's research into human activity across time and space (the "not here"), and how that research connects with contemporary everyday concerns (the "here") in complex, engaging combinations. *The Office Tower Tales* were, like *Tales for an Urban Sky*, at least in part "spawned" by Major's "life in office towers, malls, and coffee shops" ("Preface," *Urban Sky* 7), but in scope, they go well beyond that collection.

Major's *The Office Tower Tales* join in a tradition, a pattern, if you will, of disparate stories set within narrative frames that map the themes and connections onto each other. Obvious well-known predecessors include Chaucer's *Canterbury Tales*, and *The Arabian Nights Entertainment (A Thousand and One Nights)*. In the first, medieval English pilgrims pass through the April springtime on a pilgrimage to Canterbury Cathedral to the shrine for St. Thomas à Becket. For their mutual profit and delight they share stories often focused on matters of love, marriage, and morality. In the second, a collection largely of Middle Eastern and Indian stories, Scheherazade becomes queen to a misogynistic king who marries a new queen each day, then executes her at the end of their night together. Scheherazade extends her life and ends her husband's rampage by entertaining him with a new story each night, leaving the story incomplete so she needs to come back to finish it the next night, then begin a new one.

Like Chaucer, Major begins in April. Three women convene at their coffee breaks and lunches, and together over the nine-month span of *The Office Tower Tales* gestate a collective experience of the problems faced by women in the modern world. The three companions who conduct their "long debate" (2) are named openly for and invite comparison with women from classical myth and story: Pandora, the angry, unhappy, and frightened woman from accounting, who decries the uneven power arrangements between men and women, arrangements that deny opportunity and dignity to women; Aphrodite, the generally more accommodating, sexually adventurous, and forgiving woman from reception, who observes that things seem to be getting better, and who wonders if merely putting women into management would make things any better for women down the ladder; and Sheherazad [*sic*], from public relations. True to her name and occupation, Sheherazad has a storehouse of tales and anecdotes "that arise from some deep cauldron... / ...like pilgrims seeking meaning" (13), stories from across the globe and across time to bring to bear on the discussion in the here and now.

The Office Tower Tales, with its community of three communicants, illustrates Major's understanding of how language serves empathy, which she spells out in "Points on the Line": "As human beings, we can't help but understand a piece of communication as coming *from* someone *to* someone. It therefore takes place in time and in space; it is an action with consequences" (76). As analogy, illumination, or a leap of association, the stories Sheherazad tells test her understanding of the issues raised in the Prologues that frame them—they are an extended experience in empathy for the three companions, and for Major's readers.

Such is the case with "The Office Romeo's Tale," "Office Romeo" being another allusive metaphor. Major engages readers through a supernatural force that has migrated from elsewhere, another "not here," brought to bear on a problem that is both local and widely commonplace elsewhere in human experience and history: the question of what keeps men in line in their relationships with women. Major returns to Mayan myth to give Sheherazad a partial answer in Xtabay, the female ensnarer. This female power figure is a dangerous seductress whose task it is to punish male malfeasance. In the form of a recently arrived young woman from Mexico, she visits a northern prairie office Christmas party and Romeo's private office. There she becomes part of a humiliating vision that frightens the would-be seducer back into a momentary semblance of fidelity.

Such solutions, like stories, myths, and scientific processes, migrate across time and distance through the fertile patterning imagination of Alice Major. They emerge as metaphoric connections to further her readers' experience of empathy. They shine as a magpie's invitations to connection and reconnection through a collection of glittery objects patterned into further glittering objects inviting that kick, or click, of recognition.

Works Cited

Major, Alice. *Intersecting Sets: A Poet Looks at Science*. Edmonton: University of Alberta Press, 2011. Print.

———. "The Magpie's Eye." *Intersecting Sets: A Poets Looks at Science* ix-xvi.

———. *Memory's Daughter*. Edmonton: University of Alberta Press, 2010. Print.

———. "Messages from Planet E." *The Occupied World* 90.

———. "Metaphor at Play." *Intersecting Sets: A Poet Looks at Science* 17-46.

———. *The Occupied World*. Edmonton: University of Alberta Press, 2006. Print.

———. "The Office Romeo's Tale." *The Office Tower Tales* 61-68.

———. *The Office Tower Tales*. Edmonton: University of Alberta Press, 2008. Print.

———. "The Poetry Fan." *Writing the City: Poets Laureate of Edmonton, 2005-2013*. Ed. Douglas Barbour. Edmonton: Edmonton Arts Council, 2012. 11-13. Print.

———. "Points on the Line." *Intersecting Sets: A Poet Looks at Science* 67-92.

———. "A Superposition of Brains." Provost's Lecture Series. Stony Brook University, New York. 14 Nov. 2013. Lecture.

———. *Tales for an Urban Sky*. Fredericton, NB: Broken Jaw Press, 1999. Print.

———. "That Frost Feeling." *Intersecting Set: A Poet Looks at Science* 1-15.

———. "Zeno's Paradox." *Standard candles*. Edmonton: University of Alberta Press, 2015. 122. Print.

The Office Tower Tales (excerpt)

PROLOGUE TO THE OFFICE ROMEO'S TALE

The city picnic table is fraught with sparrows
as sunlight spreads its crumpled lunch bag
- yellow egg salad on brown. Elm trees
and poplar are running up green flags -
summer's bunting.

Coveys of secretaries, cotton-frocked,
are lured outdoors to corner parks
by the season's fresh jollity. Giggle
after giggle of girls. Squirrels dart
at opportunities

in the shadow of leaves. A sparrow lights
on Aphrodite's arm, cocky courtier,
bright-eyed as the young, sun-visored knights
of the road construction crew
who lounge at ease

in battered helmets and fluorescent vests
on grassy cushions, whistle mating calls.
Go away! Aphrodite suggests
pertly to the sparrow. But he perches
as if enthralled

by her sandwich. *They always come to you,*
Pandora muses, drawing in a breath of spring
like smoke from a cigarette.
Sparrow flicks a careless wing
at the obvious.

A businessman ambles by, dark jacket slung
from his fingers' crook'd peg,
a shadow in the garden. He passes among
the lunchers, beside a blonde girl
in fetching denim.

Hi, Norm! Aphrodite twitters.
He hoists his jowls in a smile and nods
towards their table with its litter
of wrappings. Pandora pointedly
turns her back.

What's YOUR problem? wonders Aphrodite,
watching while the manager escorts
his leggy young companion, politely
protective past the raucous guerdon
in their hard hats.

Pandora scowls downward at her sandwich.
Don't you know that story? she answers loudly,
sending out her voice like an officer
of the law against the jocund, rowdy,
squawking bachelors.

Four clerks from the company downstairs
got fired last week, because
they were passing pornographic pictures
on their e-mail. Pandora's jaws
clamp a crust

fiercely. She swigs her orange crush,
continues. *But that guy, Norm,*
do they give him the boot? Nope. Gosh,
he's the manager. But he's the one
who downloads stuff

in the first place. Two girls cut loose
from paycheques, but he's still sitting pretty.
Sheherazad puts down her box of juice.
Girls? she asks, astonished.
Exchanging porn?

Aphrodite shades her eyes and gazes
past the flexing pecs of the construction crew
at the dark jacket. *Norm Januarius?*
Her face perplexed. *Why would he do*
something like that?

And why did the company get straight-laced
about some sexy pictures? It's not as if
they take up any more computer space
than those photos of her kids that Zoe
keeps sending round.

Sheherazad still looks stunned.
She doesn't really like pornography –
pictures of women degraded, caparisoned
in leather. They stick, take up too much
space in her head.

Aphrodite's cheeky sparrow pecks
merrily at their leftovers. Pandora
still frowns after Norm. *Men want power and sex,*
she states. *And the more that they want power,*
the more they crave

sex too. Look at all those presidents
who can't keep their pants up.
As one who holds these truths to be self-evident,
she shuts her eyes against rebuttal.
Sparrow moves

on her crust. *Oh, get real.* Aphrodite sweeps
crumbs from the splintered, sun-scarred surface
of their picnic table. A heap
of small birds joyfully converges,
cheeping and cheerful.

Lots of guys want sex who couldn't care
a button for promotion.
Impartially, she superintends
the sparrows' plump commotion.
Take my Claudio

for example. As long as he can bang
dents out of car doors, he doesn't need
to rule the world. And there are presidents
whose dicks are nearly atrophied
for lack of use.

So sex and power are NOT *the same.*
Pandora shakes her head. *Well, maybe not*
exactly. She eyes a squirrel issuing
furious challenges - a furry Lancelot
tilting at rivals.

But they're like trees so close together
that a squirrel running up the trunk of one
is jumping in the branches of the other.
From the sun-split junctures overhead
the squirrels utter

ultimatums and rapid-fire rebukes.
Tsit-tsit-tsit. Tsit-tsit … cheet-cheet-cheat.
Their tails arch like indignant coat-hooks
for their dark jackets. They have a flare
for the dramatic.

But even then, power cuts both ways,
says Aphrodite. *I remember when*
I was in this meeting taking notes.
There were three men
in the room

and I'd had sex with all of them.
They could talk of quality improvement
all day long. But I knew more
about their product movement
than they knew.

I had as much power over them
as they had over me. She suddenly
realizes what she's let out of the lunch bag
and adds apologetically,
I wasn't married

at the time. A pink suffusion
blooms on her face. She looks down to hide
this token of clandestine confusion.
Don't ever mention this to Claudio,
she murmurs

as though a hammer-hauling husband
is hulked jealously behind a tree,
mistrustful and cudgelled.
Pandora sighs elaborately. *See?*
That's what I mean.

That's not power – something that you sneak
around with. Something you have to keep
hidden in a pocket. Only the weak
do that. Look at that guy Norm.
Scorn scores her voice.

He doesn't have to keep his trophies
secret. He puts them on display
at lunch time. Aphrodite laughs.
But that's his daughter, May,
He dotes on her.

Taken by surprise, Pandora turns
to watch the couple pacing on the grass,
safely past the tilting males. *And anyway*
adds Aphrodite, *Norm's wife would have his ass*
if he played around.

Sheherazad shivers. *And yet he downloads porn.*
Pictures of some girl his daughter's age.
Her silver moonlet swivels, forms
a question mark suspended from
one whorled ear.

What keeps males in line at all?
it seems to ask. The question walks the path
past the jousting squirrels, the wall
of wolf-whistling workers, the billowing
skirts of girls,

past the traffic of sparrows, immersed
in twittering transactions. The question
crosses into the shadow of Commerce
Place, enters the castle's raised portcullis,
makes its way

to the acreage of a desk. Meanwhile
Aphrodite gathers up the wreckage
of wrappings for the trashcan, turns to smile
at her friends. *Tell us a story, Sherry,*
she suggests.

Sheherazad squints, trying to think,
until a short, red-headed man strolls by
with a squirrel-eyed girl. She grins,
glances at her wristwatch
and begins.

The Office Romeo sidles through the crowd
drinks held aloft like a flamenco dancer
heisting castanets, ice cubes clicking.
Up front the microphone is fuzzy
with the corporate officers' annual address –
fourth-quarter profits and official
Christmas oratory. Those in line
with the speaker's eye clutch their highballs
and nod as if they're grateful.

But at the room's perimeter, no-one's paying
much attention. The office Romeo homes in
on the wedge of secretaries by the entry.
They all wear pretty dresses
for this festivity – shoulder and cleavage
displayed all day at desks,
even if the air outside is Arctic.

He proffers a glass to the new girl
from Lands and Properties. "So,
welcome to the company." His smile
comes on.

> Oh, the girl from
> Lands and Properties
> is something else. A samba
> about to start.
> A tiny, perfect body.
> Hair a fall
> of glossy water.
> A white dress, printed
> with green leaves
> across her shoulder

down her curved back,
a large leaf curling
like a hand
to cup her hip.

The Office Romeo glows like a cartoon lightbulb
turned on. His pink shirt shines. His wide tie
with the Porky Pig design loosens and falls.
He smoothes his forelock boyishly aside.

He's the bright young man of accounts
payable. His office has real walls.
He keeps a calculator on his desk
and dabs its keys with the end of his pen,
like a chicken pecking corn.

The girls are laughing. *There he goes again,*
they tell each other. *Remember when*
Anita found the socks below his desk
the morning after last year's party?
                    Oh, he's hopeless,
Christina mutters sourly. Two years ago
her earring made the morning-after news,
found on his tightly woven carpet. She still can feel
the rough scrub of rug burn her shoulders.

But the girl from lands and properties
is gazing at him, dark eyes receptive
as film in a camera just waiting for light.
He finds out she's from Mexico. *Wow,*
he breathes. *I just love May-hee-ko.*
Go there every year. Cancun's the greatest ...
do you come from there?

The girl from Lands and Properties replies
she's from Yucatan, but not Cancun.
Her home is further inland. Has he heard
of *Chichen Izta?* He shakes his head.
That's not a beach, is it? Those beaches
at Cancun are awesome. And the babes.
He's lost in reminiscence. The candy towers
along Kuculcan Avenue, the beachside bars
and pools, the hotels with marble caverns
for foyers, the packages with everything
included. He's lyric on the night at Señor Frog's,
how drunk he got on tequila, nearly croaked,
ate the worm at the bottom of the bottle
on a bet, threw up in a bed
of flowers. Oh, man, it was terrific.

So now I call you Señor Frog, she says
and for a blinking moment he thinks
she might be making fun of him
but her eyes are connecting with his
like a laser beam with a compact disk,
and he knows he'll like the music.

The official hospitality winds down,
most of the older guys head home. But the young
and party-hearty ones form wavering parades
to the pub nearby, prop themselves
at breast-high tables round the dance floor.
Waitresses squeeze by with baskets
of complimentary popcorn. Trays of drinks
sway overhead like palm trees in a breeze.

The Office Romeo is on the floor
already, strutting his shiny boots,
shaking his shoulders, throwing back his head

so his red hair sprays up. *Look at him,*
the girls perched high on barstools giggle.
He looks like a rooster revving up.

> The girl from Lands
> and Properties
> dances the same
> sway-rhythm
> to every song,
> neat swing of hips
> that somehow
> always keeps the beat,
> arms held
> close to breasts.
> She looks cool
> in spite of heat

steaming from the Office Romeo. *Let me get you
a drink* he gasps as the last chords fade.

So, what's your name again?
She sips her daiquiri, leaves no lipstick stain
on the sugary rim. *I'm called Xtabay.*

Ishta Bay? He leans earnestly against
the bar to show that he's intense
and sensitive as well. *That's different. Is that,
like, the name of some beach?*

She smiles, says it's a Mayan name
from long ago. *Oh, Mayan,* he says vaguely.
Cool. So have you got a boyfriend?
Her face looks sad. *No,
the one I had got sick.*

Further down the bar, the other girls
are a flowery spectrum of observers.
Shóuldn't someone warn her? Jasmin asks.
He's just looking to get laid, says Rosa
philosophically. *You know a cock is gonna crow*
when the sun comes up. You know Ricky there
will try and score at the Christmas party.
He isn't complicated. She's got him figured out.

Christina's fist closes on her glass. *Some day,*
someone's going to give him AIDS, she hisses,
viciously optimistic. *Oh, come on,* says Rosa.
he's harmless. He'll grow up eventually.

Some don't. Elinor's the older one,
the payroll supervisor. She lost a lot of weight
after the divorce. *Some just never learn*
unless they're forced to.

Meanwhile, the Office Romeo is feeling
fuzzier all the time, tequila sunrise sliding down
as though it's sunset on Montego Bay.
But they must be having a great conversation
the way she leans toward him. He seems to hear
I like your voice ... bet you can sing ... oh, the way
your hips move ... Though really she's just gazing
with those amazing eyes, intent.
He hazily congratulates himself. You don't
just get lucky. It's good management.

So it's hardly any time until the deejay
spins his last disk and they're slipping back
across the street – he's going to show her
his calculator or something,
he's forgotten who suggested what.

She's stepping
through snowflakes
in her sandals.
Never a shiver,
as if it's a drift
of sparkling petals
for her painted toes.

The elevator sags to a stop.
The Office Romeo steps out. *Welcome
to Bean Counter Central,* he intones
with a miscalculated flourish
that barks his knuckles on the wall.

Beans? She looks puzzled and then gleams –
a smile for something funny he can't see.
He pecks the secret code on plastic buttons
beside the doorknob, bows her in.

Cubicles and desks are dimly lit
by red exit lights and streetlamp glow
beyond the windows. The shadows
suddenly look lively, as Xtabay
sways past them to the door
with Ricky's name tacked up
on a plastic plaque.

She slides her coat off
awkwardly, like something foreign
she's not used to, looks around the room
for somewhere to put it. Her skin,
so golden in the bar
now shines white and phosphorescent
in the snowlight shimmer. The Office Romeo
feels suddenly like he's not quite so sure
where to put himself.

I gotta take a leak, he mumbles,
Be right back. By the urinal, he shakes
drops from his wilted wonder, and wonders
if he hasn't had a drink or two too much.

Coming back along the corridor, he hears
the girl from Lands and Properties. She's singing
something soft, exotic and she's moving
round his office, touching walls, caressing
corners. He shuts the door, pulls off
his tie. *Here, let me show you ...*

But it's her who's
showing him,
leaf-printed dress slipping
from one shoulder
hair straying
in a dark web across
a breast so awfully
white

The Office Romeo feels very short
of breath; his pants have dropped
around his knees. How did his belt
come unbuckled? His shirt is flapping at
his backside, his backside is flapping
at the window, and he's backing up
not sure why, except he's feeling
clammy and her breath is suddenly
sour as a hangover.

She touches his chest
with a forefinger
that now seems all nail.

Sharp pain rips round
his heart and something's
going swimmy
with his eyes. Beyond
her shoulder, vines
are sprouting up the wall.
His desk has turned
into the surface of a pond
and frogs are popping
on and off the lily pads
like a squad
of croaking cheerleaders.

I dddon't think I wwwant to... he stutters
like a calculator with a stuck key.

The room erupts.
It's full of branches. Startled eyes
stare out at him ... stare at his shorts
embroidered with the playboy bunny,
stare at his pallid legs poking
from brown socks, his palpitating chest
He's netted round with leaves,
his groin feels like bark
is growing over it.

Beans, he thinks she's saying.

No, no... he whimpers, hopping
sideways, hobbled by his trousers,
towards his desk. The leaping frogs
are still there, but so's his calculator.
He grabs it as he falls and holds it up
as though the talismanic cross of numbers
on its plastic face might have some feeble power.

But he only seems to hear a scornful comment.
Good management!

No, look I'm sorry. He's trying
to get his pants pulled up but
they're dissolving into leaves and
his shirt's becoming straw.
I'll never do it again.

One extra-large frog bops up
from the pond-desk, splats against his chest,
knocks him on his back. She's looming
over him, breath like rotting sewage
and he's paddling backwards
frantically, pushing his feet against the carpet
feeling his shoulders burn.
Oh, let me go... he whimpers.
*You're gorgeous, but I must have left
the wrong impression. I've got this girlfriend,
her name's Christina...*

There's a pause, as though the frogs
have stopped mid-jump, and for a moment
the room turns ordinary again – just one
small woman in a white dress, staring
down at him, surprised. Just a flash,
but time enough for Ricky
to reach his feet and wrench
the door open, before the frog cacophony
starts up again.

He flees the hallway – no time to wait
for elevators, and anyway
vines are bursting from the bulging shaft
and walls are quaking with demonic laughter.

He gallops to the stairwell, down ten dizzy floors,
through the whirl of revolving doors
into the street.

> In his shorts. Without
> his shoes or wallet.
> No castanet of keys
> to car or condo.
> And it's cold, cold
> December.

Ricky's teeth ache. His love life passes
before his eyes. He starts to wonder, humbly,
if he can remember
Christina's number.

EDEN ROBINSON occupies a central place in Indigenous writing today. A member of the Haisla and Heiltsuk First Nations, Robinson was born in 1968 and grew up in Kitamaat territory with her older brother and younger sister. She moved to pursue a fine arts degree at the University of Victoria, and from there, she went to Vancouver to find employment that would also provide her with the freedom to write. Robinson worked several odd jobs before having one of her short stories published in *PRISM International*. This success encouraged her to enroll in a graduate program at the University of British Columbia, where she earned a master's degree in creative writing. Her first book, *Traplines* (Knopf, 1996), is a collection of short stories that introduced the Canadian literary scene to Robinson's trademark biting humour. *Traplines* was awarded Britain's Winifred Holtby Memorial Prize, awarded to the best regional work by a Commonwealth writer. Her second book, and first novel, *Monkey Beach* (Vintage Canada, 2000), won the Ethel Wilson Fiction Prize in 2001 and was shortlisted for both the 2000 Giller Prize and the 2000 Governor General's Award for English-language fiction. Her third book, *Blood Sports*, which borrows from a story in *Traplines*, was published by McClelland & Stewart in 2006. In 2010, Robinson delivered the CLC Kreisel Lecture, *The Sasquatch at Home: Traditional Protocols & Modern Storytelling* (University of Alberta

Press/Canadian Literature Centre, 2011), wherein she discussed Haisla copyright and the intersections of family, culture, and place in storytelling. Her short fiction has been anthologized in *The Penguin Anthology of Stories by Canadian Women* (Penguin, 1997), edited by Denise Chong, as well as *So Long Been Dreaming: Postcolonial Science Fiction & Fantasy* (Arsenal Pulp Press, 2004), edited by Nalo Hopkinson and Uppinder Mehan. Robinson has been awarded the University of Victoria's Distinguished Alumni Award and has acted as a virtual writer-in-residence at the University of British Columbia's Creative Writing Program and as a writer-in-residence at the Whitehorse Public Library. Robinson and her work have received international recognition. She uses her literary celebrity at home to raise awareness for issues affecting Aboriginal peoples in Canada, such as the erosion of health care and housing availability in urban areas. Robinson continues to live and work in Kitamaat, British Columbia. Eden Robinson visited the Canadian Literature Centre to deliver her Brown Bag Lunch reading on March 19, 2014.

8

EDEN ROBINSON
Reading for B'gwus

KIT DOBSON

EDEN ROBINSON IS A DISRUPTIVE STORYTELLER. What do I
mean by that? Why "disruptive"? I mean that her mode of storytelling
disrupts, unsettles, and challenges readers. Her stylings challenge
readers' assumptions, complacencies, and habits. In a piece from
her first collection of short stories, *Traplines*, a white man asks an
Indigenous woman how he should eat the food that she offers him as
he deliberately overpays, creepily flirting with her. "With your mouth,
asshole," is the answer that she thinks before giving a straightforward
reply (208). That is, Indigenous food is eaten in the same way as
the settlers' food—except that in this context there might be an
expletive at the end, a challenge, or a disruption to what seemed like a
straightforward process of colonial consumption.

Helen Hoy uses this episode in order to frame her inquiry into
Indigenous women's writing, in her book *How Should I Read These?* I
would like to move from Hoy's recognition of the importance of the
colonial-Indigenous encounter into a reading of Eden Robinson's work
that continually disrupts the settler-Indigenous binary. I have taught
another of the short stories in *Traplines* several times, the story "Dogs
in Winter." The classroom becomes fraught whenever I teach that
text. In the story, a young woman named Lisa is coming of age against
a backdrop in which her mother is a murderer either in prison or at

large; critic Nathalie Foy reads the story as a parody of the extremes of cultural anxieties around mothering. The characters are only ever sketched in rough outlines: we know where they live in Canada, but we do not know a great deal about them. When we come together to discuss the text in class, a great deal seems to hinge upon how students have interpreted the characters. Are they Indigenous? If so, how can we tell? Some details could lead readers in that direction, but only if readers rely upon stereotypes about Indigenous people (there is, for example, prominent imagery of moose in the story that often comes up in class conversations). Sam McKegney notes, in reference to Robinson, that "that which is unseen, as that which is unspoken, poses the greatest threat" in her work (12). Whether the characters of "Dogs in Winter" are Indigenous or not is one of those unseen dimensions in Robinson's writing. The unaware reader is, indeed, one who is going to be challenged here, and being "aware" of Robinson as a writer means going well beyond any surface descriptions.

In an article that I wrote previously for the journal *Canadian Literature*, I focused primarily upon Robinson's novels, focusing on the ambivalent ways in which Indigeneity and ethnicity enter into them (56). Robinson has been clear in interviews that she would like to be considered a writer first and foremost; her status as an Indigenous person is a part of who she is, but her interactions with such labels is playful, disruptive. Her favourite author and main inspiration is Stephen King. She is very much a part of the bourgeoning world of Indigenous writing in Canada and internationally, but that very categorization is something that raises questions. For whom does the category of Indigenous writing exist? Is it a space for Indigenous people to create something new? Or, in the hands of a mainstream readership that is imagined as being predominantly white, might it be a tidy box that allows that mainstream to contain, package, and dismiss Indigenous people anew? In an interview that Smaro Kamboureli and I did with Cherokee writer Daniel Heath Justice, Justice suggested that Canada's mainstream—as well as that of the United States—tends to be most comfortable only with having a "Native writer of the moment" (87). Sometimes, it might be a well-recognized figure like Thomas King or Joseph Boyden; sometimes it could be Eden Robinson. Is such recognition enabling? Or might it curtail a broad field of expressiveness that is, undoubtedly, very much on the rise on what many Indigenous peoples term Turtle Island? Robinson doesn't let the questions end there, either; in a recent article, Sabrina Reed notes that the novel *Blood Sports* turns on the issue of moral luck in order to contemplate questions of addiction. For Reed, "Robinson omits Aboriginal markers...because otherwise her novel might be limited by her audience's assumptions about Aboriginal peoples and addiction" (160). Writing texts that at times deploy Indigenous markers and at other times hold them back allows, for instance, the inquiry into moral luck, into characters who face circumstances in which the decisions that they make are always fraught, and in which there are no simple solutions. Lydia Efthymia Roupakia writes that, even while it situates itself clearly within the terrain of an Indigenous literary tradition to which readers bring many expectations, Robinson's novel *Monkey Beach* "challenges the reader's facile recourse to established critical templates structured around perceptions of cultural authenticity, postcolonial resistance, and poststructural hybridity" (291). In other words, through a series of resistances that can be either subtle or overt, Eden Robinson's literary practice is one that seeks to challenge established reading practices. She is in the habit, as Ella Soper-Jones notes of the novel *Monkey Beach*, of "critiquing the very hermeneutic practices her representation elicits" (29).

These are but some of the questions that we might bring to bear on the book produced from Robinson's CLC Kreisel Lecture, *The Sasquatch at Home: Traditional Protocols & Modern Storytelling*. The portion of that text reproduced here, the third and final section, features one prominent absent-presence in Robinson's writing, the figure of the sasquatch. As Robinson narrates her recent time spent in and around Kitamaat in northern British Columbia, we find that she returns to two themes: the theme of which stories she might tell, and the theme of how stories are present in the land. The first theme indicates the challenge of the mainstream's perceived demand that Robinson act as a "representative" Indigenous writer, especially in the sense of a writer who represents her community. There is, she notes, a concept of "Haisla copyright" that governs her writerly choices: she is not entitled to "use any of the clan stories" because they "are owned by either individuals or families and require permission and a feast in order to be published" (31). Robinson's choices are governed, in other words, by an ethical claim that comes from her home community when she wishes to tell stories set in and around it. The concept of "ownership" is modified by its context; not all stories are fair game and she must tread wisely. In this respect, Robinson refuses the label of being a representative of her community: she does not simplistically place herself in the role of the "Native informant" who relays her community's knowledge to outsiders. In so doing, she also refuses to slide into territory that could render her the "Native writer of the moment," because her relationship to that label, "Native," is in need of so much contextual understanding.

The stories with which Robinson is concerned as a writer are nevertheless present, there in the land and all around her, in contexts that casual readers might equate with a so-called authentic or stereotypical vision of Indigeneity. Yet Robinson's interest remains the stories themselves. As she spends time at the Rediscovery Camp, learning about oxsuli from one of the elders there, and as she details her travels with her father and he tells her about each location, place emerges through narrative. The stories grow out of the interactions that she has with the land, mediated by those who share their knowledge with her. Her father is particularly taken by the sasquatch, the "b'gwus" in the Haisla language with which Robinson tells us she struggles. No one has seen a b'gwus in a long time, but her father has no trouble believing that they still exist: "they've built a mall and they're too busy driving around and shopping to visit us anymore," he jokes (39). Robinson takes his joke as being, in part, a criticism of her own life in the city, but the image is wonderful and worth dwelling upon. What if the b'gwus are up there in northern British Columbia, in the mountains and away from all people, with strip malls and F-150s? Would it be so very different from the world that urban dwellers in

Canada inhabit? The passage ends with Robinson's father joking that the sasquatches "must be at home...writing" (41). That's why they don't find any on their travels. So Robinson herself, then, is one of the sasquatches, the b'gwus who hide from the people in their cars, their malls, and the basement apartments in which they pen their novels. The b'gwus, in other words, blurs with "mainstream culture," a culture that Robinson describes herself as living in and out of as she travels to and from Kitamaat. It is the demands of this sasquatch culture that she navigates as a writer, a culture that wants to consume her as an Indigenous writer who might represent a Haisla culture that is rightfully wary of sharing its stories out of context.

In his recent nonfiction, Thomas King has suggested that contemporary Indigenous peoples are "inconvenient" to the imaginaries of settler-colonial cultures that seek a nice, tidy narrative that would allow for a simple understanding. *The Sasquatch at Home* provides a different tactic: rather than being inconvenient, Eden Robinson's stories and writing simply are. They do not need to respond to critics' and readers' desires, and therein they find their strength. There might not be any simple understanding, but that doesn't matter. Should Robinson need to be concerned with the categorical thinking and limitations that critics bring to her works? Of course not. She may wish to be accountable to the communities about which she writes, but beyond that, the challenge falls upon her readership to arrive at an ethical practice of understanding, one that readers must strive to cultivate by reading her works, and reading them with care. Her role, then, as a disruptive writer becomes clear, as she unsettles the simplistic norms and assumptions that readers may bring to her texts.

Works Cited

Dobson, Kit. "Indigeneity and Diversity in Eden Robinson's Work." *Canadian Literature* 201 (2009): 54–67. Print.

Dobson, Kit, and Smaro Kamboureli. "To Hear this Different Story: Interview with Daniel Heath Justice." *Producing Canadian Literature: Authors Speak on the Literary*

Marketplace. Kit Dobson and Smaro Kamboureli. Waterloo, ON: Wilfrid Laurier University Press, 2013. 75–91. Print.

Foy, Nathalie. "Eden Robinson's 'Dogs in Winter': Parodic Extremes of Mothering." *Textual Mothers/Maternal Texts: Motherhood in Contemporary Women's Literatures.* Eds. Elizabeth Podnieks and Andrea O'Reilly. Waterloo, ON: Wilfrid Laurier University Press, 2010. Web. 19 Jan. 2015.

Hoy, Helen. *How Should I Read These? Native Women Writers in Canada.* Toronto: University of Toronto Press, 2001. Print.

King, Thomas. *The Inconvenient Indian: A Curious Account of Native People in North America.* Toronto: Doubleday, 2012. Print.

McKegney, Sam. *Magic Weapons: Aboriginal Writers Remaking Community after Residential School.* Winnipeg: University of Manitoba Press, 2007. Print.

Reed, Sabrina. "'Just Say No': Eden Robinson and Gabor Maté on Moral Luck and Addiction." *Mosaic* 47.4 (2014): 151–66. Web. 20 Jan. 2015.

Robinson, Eden. *The Sasquatch at Home: Traditional Protocols & Modern Storytelling.* Edmonton: University of Alberta Press/Canadian Literature Centre, 2011. Print.

———. *Traplines.* Toronto: Vintage, 1996. Print.

Roupakia, Lydia Efthymia. "On Judging with Care and the Responsibility of an Heir: Reading Eden Robinson's *Monkey Beach*." *University of Toronto Quarterly* 81.2 (2012): 279–96. Web. 20 Jan. 2015.

Soper-Jones, Ella. "The Fate of the Oolichan: Prospects of Eco-Cultural Restoration in Eden Robinson's *Monkey Beach*." *Journal of Commonwealth Literature* 44.2 (2009): 15–33. Web. 20 Jan. 2015.

The Sasquatch at Home (excerpt)

(68) Veratrum viride *Ait. Ssp.* Eschscholzii
(A. Gray) Love & Love
(Indian Hellebore, or False Hellebore)
  —(HAISLA) AUX SULI

Medicine: CAUTION; HIGHLY TOXIC.
Respiratory aid; analgesic or anti-inflammatory (treatment for arthritis and other pain); hypertension and blood disorder, unspecified medicine, emetic, purgative, sedative, hemostat.

Ritual or Spiritual: *ritual medicine (shamanistic preparation, purification emetic, repel ghosts, illness, evil and witchcraft, acquisition of luck); used by bear and wolf as ritual medicine.*
  —BRIAN D. COMPTON, *"Upper North Wakashan"*

*The best known monsters of Haisla territory were the Bekwis. These were
large, hairy creatures that were reported occasionally in the Q'waq'waksiyas
shoreline area just above Bishop Bay, and for that reason it is known as
Monkey Beach. These Bekwis have come to be called Sasquatches or
"stick men" elsewhere.*

—OUR HAISLA STEWARDSHIP AREAS

The Haisla measure of intelligence is slightly different from that of
mainstream culture. Three main indicators are an ability to trace your
family roots back to mythic times, not having to be told twice and
being able to replicate an action after being shown how to do it. By
most Haisla measurements, I am "special." I can vaguely remember my
immediate family and get fuzzy on the stories. Anyone who has taught
me (or tried to teach me) Haisla knows you can tell me twenty or so
times and I might remember a word or phrase. I have a vague idea of
how to live a traditional life but would probably starve if I had to catch
and cure my own fish and berries.

I enjoyed school because it was the first place where people
considered me smart. I was much better at remembering things that
were written down and in learning from books. After high school, I
went to the University of Victoria for my Bachelor of Fine Arts and then
immediately began grad school at the University of British Columbia
for my Master of Fine Arts. I began writing my first novel as my thesis,
and then switched to a collection of short stories so that I could use my
novel as a grant application for the now defunct Explorations Program.
My thesis became my first short story collection and I immediately
began writing my novel, a coming-of-age story set on the northwest
coast.

I ran into problems early. First, the main character was a young
woman named Karaoke, about whom I'd written in a short story in the
collection called "Queen of the North." Karaoke was traumatized by
the events of the short story and lay flat on the page. Next I dithered
on whether or not to set the novel in Kitamaat Village or to emulate
Margaret Laurence and make up a place. I'd kept Karaoke in the Village

and it had been an uncomfortable experience. An entire novel seemed daunting. In the end though, the story lost its context and much of its zip when taken out of the Village so I decided to consult with my aunties on the stickier issues, like Haisla copyright.

I knew I couldn't use any of the clan stories—these are owned by either individuals or families and require permission and a feast in order to be published. Informal stories that were in the public domain, such as stories told to teach children our nuyem, could be published— unless they had information people felt uncomfortable sharing with outsiders, such as spiritual or ceremonial content. I wanted a couple of scenes at a potlatch, but wasn't sure what I'd have to do to have it included in the novel. A cousin of mine said although most traditional people were uncomfortable talking about the potlatch itself, what the people were doing or saying while the potlatch was going on was a different story. It turned out better for the story because I'd had three exposition-heavy pages that were reduced to a quick transitional paragraph, while the tensions between family members and the children playing around them, oblivious, came to the forefront.

In these early stages of writing *Monkey Beach*, I was invited to a Haisla Rediscovery Camp in the Kitlope Valley. The program sought to reconnect Haisla youth with the traditional ways of learning. If I wrote a short piece, I could participate in the program for free. I jumped at the opportunity of a working vacation that would help me nail the locations of the book. The Kitlope Valley is a remote, untouched watershed with glacier-fed rivers and high, bald mountains. The boat ride took three hours and I rode out with the elders and a dendrologist who was recording culturally modified trees. The camp included myself, some researchers, elders, camp cooks and sixteen sixteen-year-old boys. We transferred into a jet boat at the mouth of the Kitlope River because the river was too shallow for the diesel seiner to go up.

In the mornings we split into small groups and travelled the territory, learning our stories and traditional ways of living. We'd gather wild rice on a mud flat or follow animal tracks or learn about the families that had lived here before depopulation from smallpox and flu epidemics forced them to move to the main reserve. In the evening, we did chores, ate dinner and then were supposed to gather around the lakeshore for cultural sharing around a campfire so that we could teach the others in the group what we had learned that day. The boys were keenly feeling the lack of television, and the batteries for their games and Walkmen had died, so most of their cultural sharing involved recreating scenes from the recently released *Wayne's World*. By the end of two weeks, although I hadn't seen the movie yet, I could recite most of the dialogue and plot points.

The Rediscovery Camp heavily influenced the structure and content of *Monkey Beach*. Walking the territory, boating the territory, eating food I'd collected and being immersed in the stories was inspiring. My grandmother character in the book knew a lot about our traditional healing, so I was particularly interested in learning about plants and medicines. One of the elders at the camp was excited that I was interested in the old medicines and was hopeful that I would carry our knowledge to a younger generation. I asked her about oxsuli, a powerful plant more commonly known as Indian Hellebore. I'd be fascinated by it ever since one of my uncles had tried to use it to help his arthritis. He hadn't listened to the instructions for its safe use, and put an entire root bulb in his bath. Within minutes, he was paralysed and had to call his wife for help. She called the ambulance, but the paramedics couldn't lift him out of the tub. The volunteer firefighters were called in. Most of them were my uncle's high school basketball buddies, and they teased him relentlessly about getting stuck in the tub.

The elder offered to show me a place where the oxsuli were just starting to grow back. A shift in the river had wiped out the mud flats that oxsuli prefer. We took a speedboat out to the site and I tied up on shore. Oxsuli grow tall with heart-shaped elliptic leaves. The tiny greenish-yellow flowers droop from the top in tassels. The berries are highly toxic and range from beige to deep red. The oxsuli we found were only knee-high. As she touched a leaf, she told me a story about her grandmother teaching her about oxsuli just as she was teaching me. She bent over further and cleared away some dirt, exposing the root, a stringy orange cluster. I knew the root was used to keep ghosts away and for good luck, but she told me how to use the root to cure headaches.

"You should get to know its energy," she said. "Lean in and study it."

"Okay."

"I'm glad they're growing back here," she said. "They haven't for a long time."

As I leaned in to study the oxsuli, my rubber boots slipped in the mud and I fell on top of it and squashed it.

The elder was quiet as I picked myself up and tried to unsquash the plant.

"Maybe you should stick to writing," she said.

When we got back to the speedboat, we discovered I had not tied it as effectively as I thought and it was floating away up the tide.

"You tied her up," she said. "You swim out to get her."

Glaciers feed the rivers and the water is cold. I have never bathed less in my entire life than when I was at the Rediscovery Camp. I would roll out of my tent in the morning and wander down to the beach. Most of the two weeks were overcast and chilly. The mountains steamed and the mist formed columns that rose up and merged with the clouds. One morning, a great blue heron balanced on a log watching seals roll in Kitlope Lake. The lake is wide and shallow. Orcas sometimes follow the seals up the lake and their tall dorsal fins slice the water as they hunt. When Dad used to trap here, he would watch the Orcas shimmy up the rocks to grab a seal and slide back into the lake.

The Kitlope is also prime bear habitat. At the mouth of the river on the day we arrived, I saw a black bear on the shore eating seaweed. It stuck its nose in the air as we approached, then waddled into the forest. Black bear footprints were seen lacing our camp. They nosed around the meat freezer and left claw marks on nearby trees. I saw a spirit bear for the first time, a yellowish small bear in an abandoned crabapple grove.

I hoped to see my first Sasquatch or at the very least, pick up a few stories. When I was growing up, my mother used to tell us about Tony's place, an abandoned settler's farm near a lagoon on the mainland across from Bella Bella. When they were children, my mother and her siblings used to pick cherries and plums from the orchard. The farm had been abandoned suddenly—breakfast dishes were still laid out, the beds were unmade and clothes still hung from the laundry line. One of my uncles was at the stage when he was fascinated by coins and he went along the line, carefully checking the pockets with shaking hands. My mother asked him who he was afraid would catch him and he said the sasquatches who were rumoured to have attacked the settlement and carried off one of the white women.

My father said the *b'gwus*, as Sasquatch are called in Haisla, had clans and families, their own songs and feasts. In the stories that Ma-ma-oo told him when he was a child, b'gwus meant Wild Man of the Woods, and he thought they might not be ape-like creatures at all, but exiles who had been banned from their villages and had gone to live where they wouldn't be harassed and that it was loneliness and isolation that made them so strange.

The Kitlope is famously home to Sasquatch. The territory bordering on Bella Coola or Nuhalk lands is mountainous and remote. Many of the old stories passed down the generations talk about the elusive b'gwus and their lack of females. They would creep into villages and steal women who took their fancy. The last encounter was in Miskusa, across from Kemano in 1918. Billy Hall shot and killed one by mistake, thinking it was a bear. After escaping from the other b'gwus, Billy Hall gained special powers and had a mask carved to commemorate the event. Dad had known Billy Hall when he was a child and had an insatiable curiosity about Sasquatches for the rest of his life. He sought out elders and listened to their stories, committing them to memory. He was delighted when I told him I would be writing about Monkey Beach and more enthusiastic than I was to get me to the sites he knew so well.

Ma-ma-oo had a bentwood box full of traditional regalia that was only supposed to be brought out for feasts and potlatches. My father liked to bring the b'gwus mask out and tell us the story of Billy Hall. The b'gwus mask has a dance at the feasts, usually the less formal ones. They were always my favourite part of an otherwise stuffy occasion when I was growing up. All the other dances were serious and you had to be still and pay respectful attention. But when a dancer wears a Sasquatch mask and pretends to dig for clams and cockles, hiding his face shyly, the children push to the front to watch him. Then he'll spot a pretty woman in the audience and "abduct" her. For example, when Iona Campagnolo was with the Liberal Party, she was an honoured guest at the opening of the Haisla Recreation Centre. During the ceremonies, the Sasquatch dancer stopped dead when he saw her, patted his heart and pretended to drag her off, much to the delight of the audience.

| A few years later, I made it back to Monkey Beach. I'd been close at the Rediscovery Camp, but we hadn't had the time to visit. Since then, I had been holed up in my apartment in Vancouver. I was having difficulty ending the book and was in search of inspiration. When I asked Dad if he could take me there for a little research, he enthusiastically agreed—after all, he said, any book that had a Sasquatch was bound to be a bestseller.

I flew home for a week and caught up with my family. My main character zipped around in a twelve-foot speedboat with a putt-putt motor, and I had my heart set on doing the same. The weather wasn't co-operating though. The wind was fierce and Dad shook his head and told me we probably wouldn't be going. One of my younger cousins invited me to a house party. In an attempt not to appear stodgy, I drank a little too enthusiastically. When Dad shook me awake early the next morning, he said it was now or never.

I followed my father to our speedboat. The early morning air was still and cold but the sky was cloudless, promising a hot, summer day. Dad jumped down into the boat and I handed him my bags. He paused in the middle of loading.

"Do you hear that? That's *gunesella*. When an eagle makes that sound before you go hunting or fishing, it's good luck."

The unseen eagle made a trilling sound, a musical gargling.

I waited for it to appear, watching the trees behind the darkened houses that lined the semicircle of the bay. I knew I should pull out my black notebook and write this down, but I was too hungover and tired to make the effort.

The outboard motor was cranky, and Dad pulled the cord over and over before it decided to start. He cast us off. My stomach rolled. I hunched into my seat and belatedly realized that I'd left my Gravol on the kitchen counter.

I looked back as we pulled out of the bay. The Village was squashed up against the mountains and the water. Kitamaat is home to about 700 members of the Haisla nation. About 800 more live off-reserve. We're almost back to our pre-contact population of 2,000. Even with the people we have, the housing shortage is acute. New subdivisions have expanded almost to the boundaries of the reserve.

The speedboat skipped across the Douglas Channel. We're seventy miles from the open ocean. The mountains enclose the channel on either side, steep walls of trees and rocks. The shore is a thick brown line against the green of trees and the dark, dark blue of the channel.

It took us two hours to get to Monkey Beach. When he stopped the motor and oared us ashore, I was disappointed. My childhood memories made it seem much larger than this tiny cove. I noted the whiteness of the sand, made up, he tells me, of ground-up shells. I wandered around, swatting away mosquitoes, horseflies and no-see-ums. Dad pulled out his camcorder.

My brother had told me about a white man who brought gorillas to the Douglas Channel and they escaped, and terrorized people until the winter killed them off. I asked Dad if that's why it's called Monkey Beach. He shook his head. "The Haisla name is Awamusdis, the beach of plenty. There's three different kind of clams and two different kind of cockles. We used to use this beach like our freezer in the winter. Sasquatches dig for cockles here. It's their favourite food."

Long ago, he told me, some Haisla people were camping on the beach. When they woke up, the sacks of cockles they'd collected were emptied, the shells sucked clean. Footprints, large and strange, trailed into the woods. That night, they heard it, a howl not quite wolf, not quite human.

"You don't see them around any more. Some people say they're extinct," Dad said. "But they're not. They're up in the mountains somewhere, and they've built a mall and they're too busy driving around and shopping to visit us anymore."

"Where do you dig for clams and cockles?" I asked, ignoring the jibe.

"Around the point," he said, "the south side of the beach."

My running shoes sank into the soft sand as I made my way to the other side of the beach. I clambered over logs. The sand gave way to slippery, barnacle-covered rocks.

Ah, I thought, when I reached the point. The rest of the beach stretched away until it disappeared behind another point. The tide was too high to reach the south side. I stopped, shivering, excited, already rewriting scenes in my head: Morning light slanted over the mountains as a raven croaks in the trees. An otter bobbed in the kelp, rolled lazily onto its back, then watched me with its hands folded over its belly. A weasel slithered through the logs and hurried into the trees. I took my disposable panoramic camera out of my pocket and began snapping pictures. Dad joined me and I took a photograph of him videotaping me.

We spent the day wandering around the area. I could point to any mountain, any river or any rocky shoreline and he knew the history. Dad especially liked to retell the story of T'ismista, the man who turned to stone. When you are on Kitlope Lake, looking up at the mountain, there is a looming, dark stone figure looking back down at you. That was Henkwa. He lived up on the flats at the top of the lake. One day he called his two dogs to his canoe and started paddling. He went past the bluff that was the place where the Henaaksiala taught their young men to "master the mountains" so they could climb up to get goats. He passed Ago'yewa on the other side of the lake, to the place where the Rediscovery Camp was in 1996. He went a little further and then turned and crossed the lake, beaching his canoe on the east side of the lake just below Ago'yewa. When he got out of the canoe, he left a footprint in the rock on the beach. The footprint is large and easily seen. You can also see the dog prints and the thin line of his spear dragging on the ground beside him. When he climbed up the mountain, he got stuck on one of the steep cliff edges and froze. He couldn't go up and he couldn't go down. In the end, he turned to stone. If you follow his trail up to visit him, be careful. Many people puke blood or get sick and it is rumoured to be bad luck to go too near him. A helicopter tour trying to take pictures of him crashed into Kitlope Lake once....

When Dad was fishing in Kemano, he had been hired by an elder to take them out on the land while she gave nusa to a young hereditary chief, her grandson. As part of his training he was supposed to know his land and all the stories, the history of his clan, his villages and their neighbours. They'd spent days doing exactly what we were doing, bumping around in a small boat. Dad told me stories that she had told her grandson as I scribbled them down in my notebook. My favourite is the one where clams have black tongues because in the beginning, the world was on fire and they tried to put it out by spitting.

As we got ready to leave, I said, "No hungry Sasquatches here today."

"They must be at home," Dad says with a smile, "writing."

GREGORY SCOFIELD is a Métis poet, playwright, educator, and social worker of Cree, European, and Jewish ancestry. He was born in 1966 in Maple Ridge, British Columbia. He combines oral storytelling, spoken word, song, and the Cree language in his work and reading style to create a unique and powerful oeuvre. Scofield's work draws heavily from his personal experience, exploring themes and topics as diverse as family history, street life, poverty, and racial identity. He has been an important community leader in the realm of Indigenous gay literature and activism, creating, through his writing, an open space for the recognition and celebration of all sexualities. His first poetry collection, *The Gathering: Stones for the Medicine Wheel* (Polestar, 1993), was awarded the Dorothy Livesay Prize in 1994. He followed up this collection with *Native Canadiana: Songs from the Urban Rez* (Polestar, 1996), and *Love Medicine and One Song* (Kegedonce Press, 1997, 2009), in which the Cree language plays a particularly important role. He remembers the lives of his mother and aunts in *I Knew Two Métis Women: The Lives of Dorothy Scofield and Georgina Houle Young* (Polestar, 1999; Gabriel Dumont Institute of Native Studies and Applied Research, 2009). *Thunder Through My Veins: Memories of a Métis Childhood* (Flamingo, 1999) is an autobiographical work of prose that explores many of the themes present in his poetry.

Scofield's fifth collection, *Singing Home the Bones* (Raincoast, 2005), was also the title given to the documentary *Singing Home the Bones: A Poet Becomes Himself* (The May Street Group, 2006), which follows Scofield's investigation of his ancestry after discovering his father was Jewish. He has also published *kipocihkân: Poems New & Selected* (Nightwood Editions, 2009), and his most recent collection is *Louis: The Heretic Poems* (Nightwood Editions, 2011). As an outreach worker in Vancouver, he worked with street youth before teaching First Nations and Métis literature at Brandon University. He has also taught at the Emily Carr Institute, has been the writer-in-residence at Memorial University, and was the inaugural writer/storyteller-in-residence at the University of Manitoba's Centre for Creative Writing and Oral Culture. The CBC has produced two of his radio dramas, "Follow the Buffalo Home" and "The Storyteller." Scofield currently resides in Sudbury, Ontario. Gregory Scofield visited the Canadian Literature Centre to deliver his Brown Bag Lunch reading on December 1, 2010.

9

GREGORY SCOFIELD

kistêyihtamowin êkwa sâkihitowin (Honour and Love)

ANGELA VAN ESSEN

I AM LEARNING TO SPEAK nêhiyawêwin (the Cree language);
a language Métis poet Gregory Scofield breathes, sings, prays, and
laughs in throughout much of his work. I began this journey in part
to try to understand my relationship to the place I grew up in, the
city my father's family immigrated to in 1953. What does it mean
to live in Edmonton, in Treaty 6 territory? What does it mean for a
mistikwaskisin-iskwêw (Dutch woman) to learn nêhiyawêwin? This
journey has humbled and delighted me time and again. As I learn, the
more I realize how the rhythm of nêhiyawêwin is unlike the rhythm
of English. It reminds me of learning a new kind of dance: when you
are learning a new dance, you need to learn how to step; so too when
you are learning a language—you need to learn where the emphasis
falls. Here is an example: kistâpitêho—the *â* (marked by a circumflex)
is long, so you hold it longer than a short vowel—this is where your
foot hovers for a moment before coming down on the "pit": kistâ-
pit-êho. Now here is a related word: kistâpitêhotân. Now the step, the
emphasis, changes to keep the rhythm: this time your foot hovers
above the ground with the long *ê* and comes down in a fluid motion
with the hotân: *kis*-tâpi-*tê*-hotân. Doesn't the rhythm in these two
little words make you want to start dancing? Can you feel the rhythm
in your feet? I can try to describe or teach you about the rhythm and

the sounds of Cree (would it help if I told you that the emphasis often falls on the antepenultimate syllable?), but if you are not familiar with nêhiyawêwin, you need to *hear* the words in order for them to come alive.

Richard Van Camp claims that "when you're reading Gregory Scofield, yes, it's a poem, but it's also a song" (Pryor). In many of Scofield's poems, the rhythm and the music come from nêhiyawêwin. This becomes clear when you hear him perform his poetry, particularly works like "Oh Dat Agnes" or "Prayer Song for the Returning of Names and Sons," which feature Cree speakers, Cree words, and Cree song. (If you have not had the pleasure of hearing Scofield perform his poetry in person, you can see and hear him perform many of his works in the documentary *Singing Home the Bones: A Poet Becomes Himself*. The Gabriel Dumont Institute has also published an edition of *I Knew Two Métis Women* that includes two audio CDs featuring Scofield, along with other musicians and actors, performing each of the poems in the book as well as the musical intertexts.)

Scofield's work teaches us that speaking nêhiyawêwin (or any language, for that matter) is a bodily act, a sensual act. In his poem "I'll Teach You Cree," the speaker says, "with the tip of my spring tongue, ayîki [frog] / your mouth will be the web /catching apihkêsis words [spider]" (*kipocihkân* 141). The imagery here suggests that learning to speak a language puts you into an intimate relationship with the first-language speaker because it means that you will learn to put your tongue where a native speaker puts his tongue. It means you will try to make your lips do what her lips do. You will try to make your breath move through your voice box, your mouth, your lips in the same way his does. In honouring the language in this way, the student nourishes the teacher: "your mouth," the speaker says, "will be the branches / I am picking clean" (141).

The imagery here points at a mutual relationship between the native speaker and the student, and at the same time, the relationship is also intimately connected to creation, to the land. The images evoke relationships among the humans and plant life (saskatoons), animal life (frogs, spiders, dogs, and beavers), and the land itself (through references to seasons, moons, and making camp). In this way, Scofield's work explores the Cree concept of wâhkôhtowin (roughly translated can mean "relationships"), which is always mindful of "all my relations"—relations that include but are not limited to human relations. As the Cree Elder George Brertton explains in the short film *Wahkohtowin: The Relationship between Cree People and Natural Law*, "when we talk about wâhkôhtowin, you know it's that we're related." He goes on to say that everything is "part of the earth, just like we are" and our relationship with and reliance on the earth and all of creation humble us. In his interview with Sam McKegney, Scofield explains how the land, ceremonies, and our bodies are "all interconnected. The muskeg, the reeds, the rocks, the smell of the earth, the bogs, all of these things are medicines from the earth, and those are things that we possess within our own bodies" (220). We can see here how Scofield's poetry is deeply imbued with aspects of Cree and Métis world view, and his love poetry explores a Cree understanding of sâkihitowin (love), where, as Warren Cariou points out, love "is an entire way of thinking about people's relations with each other and with the world. It connects bodily experience with spiritual experience, and it is fundamentally about responsibility as well: our responsibility to each other and to the natural world that is the source of our sustenance" (Cariou iv). The word *sâkihitowin* features the morpheme *ito*, which, I am told, suggests reciprocity. So the word means mutual love, and is always therefore grounded in a concept of balanced relations. But when I hear this word, *sâkihitowin*, I hear another word echoed in it: *sâkipakâwipîsim*, leaf budding moon. It reminds me of that vibrant green you see in spring when the leaves begin to sprout. So the word, to me, echoes in creation, and reminds me that love, when it is understood in the context of wâhkôhtowin, is more than a mutual love between two human beings; it bursts forth from all our relations. We see this sort of love budding out of the images in Scofield's poem "I've Been Told," in which heaven is a place where the poplar trees are forever in bloom and there is always room for new arrivals.

Scofield's understanding of sâkihitowin seems to be closely linked to kistêyihtamowin, the nêhiyaw concept of honour. Neal McLeod, a leading nêhiyaw scholar and poet, first drew my attention to this word, and showed me how, if you look closely, it can be broken down into three morphemes: *kistê* has to do with importance, *yihta* has to do with thought, and *mowin* is the nominalizer for transitive inanimate verbs. Put back together the word suggests that honour means thinking that something is important, that you honour something with your thoughts. Scofield seeks to think highly and deeply about his relations, and his poetry honours these relations. Many of his works focus on his relationships with okâwiya (his mother), okâwîsa (his aunty, or "little mother"), and his other human relatives. In his poem "Prayer Song for the Returning of Names and Sons," included in this anthology, the speaker invokes and invites his ancestors into conversation and relationship. Indeed, he does so through song, through prayer. So when Van Camp declares that "when you're reading Gregory Scofield, yes, it's a poem, but it's also a song, but most of all, when you read Gregory Scofield, you've entered into ceremony," he is gesturing towards the way Scofield's poetry, like Cree ceremony, invokes relationships with ancestors and the spirit world, our whole selves (body, mind, spirit, and emotions), creation and the land, and with other human beings (Pryor).

Scofield's work is profoundly celebratory. He honours and elevates that which has been denigrated (for example, human sexuality, particularly gay male sexuality; or women, particularly Cree and Métis women) into the realm of the sacred. In his interview with Sam McKegney, Scofield talks about his approach to sexuality and the sacred in his work. He recalls how the lines "my mouth / the lodge where you come / to sweat" (from his poem "Ceremonies" in *Love Medicine*) came to him while he was reflecting on Cree ceremony, particularly those of the matotisân (sweat lodge). At first he thought, "I can't write that because that's taking a sacred ceremony and sexualizing it" (221-22). However, upon reflection he came to think, "the sweat is a sacred purification. It's the womb. It's the womb of Mother Earth. You're being born and you come out. And what I'm describing is just as much a ceremony, is just as sacred" (222).

Scofield brings his understanding of Cree ceremony and teachings to bear on all aspects of his life, and then lets them loose on the world through his poetry. When I read his work, the word that comes to my mind is *kistêyihtamowin*, honour. Scofield's poems honour the complexities of human existence in all our human parts: emotional, physical, spiritual, and mental. And his work is also deeply relational, so that he honours his relationships with the land, his ancestors, his lovers, and the narratives that have shaped him. His work calls for readers and audience members to reflect on their own relationships with themselves, ancestors, lovers, and the places that they call home.

Author's Note

kinanâskomitinâwâw nitokiskinohamâkêmak Dorothy Thunder, Reuben Quinn, Louis Bird, Tomson Highway, Louise Halfe, êkwa Neal McLeod. ayi-hay! Special thanks to Reuben for always emphasizing and explaining correct articulation, and for teaching me some of the layers of the word *sâkihitowin*; its connection to *sâkipakâw*, askiy, mîna mîtosak. kitatamihin.

Works Cited

Cariou, Warren. "Circles and Triangles: Honouring Indigenous Erotica." Introduction to *Love Medicine and One Song/Sâkihitowin-Maskihkiy Êkwa Pêyak-Nikamowin/* ᓵᑭᐦᐃᑐᐃᐧᐣ ᒫᐢᑭᐦᑭᕀ ᐁᑿ ᐯᔭᐠ ᓂᑲᒧᐃᐧᐣ. 2nd ed. Wiarton, ON: Kegedonce, 2009. Print.

McKegney, Sam. "A Liberation through Claiming: A Conversation with Gregory Scofield." *Masculindians: Conversations about Indigenous Manhood.* Winnipeg: University of Manitoba Press, 2014. 213–21. Print.

Pryor, Hilary, dir. *Singing Home the Bones: A Poet Becomes Himself*. Interviews and Performances by Gregory Scofield, Patrick Lane, and Richard Van Camp. The May Street Group, 2006. DVD.

Scofield, Gregory. *I Knew Two Métis Women: The Lives of Dorothy Scofield and Georgina Houle Young.* Saskatoon: Gabriel Dumont Institute of Native Studies and Applied Research, 2009. Print and Audio CDs.

———. *kipocihkân: Poems New & Selected.* Gibsons, BC: Nightwood Editions, 2009. Print.

Skidmore, Lese, dir. *Wahkohtowin: The Relationship between Cree People and Natural Law.* Elder Interviews and Discussion by William Dreaver, Isaac Chamakese, George Brertton, and Fred Campiou. Translator: Gilman Cardinal. Edmonton: Bear Paw Media, 2009. DVD.

kipocihkân: Poems New & Selected (excerpt)

PRAYER SONG FOR THE RETURNING OF NAMES AND SONS

YA-HEY-YA-HO

YA-HEY-YA-HEY

YA-HEYA

YA-HEY-HEY-YO

HIYA-HEY

HEY-HI-YA-HEY

YA-HEYA

YA-HEY-HEY-YO

HIYA-HEY

YA-HEY-YA-HEYA

YA-HEY-HEY-YO

HEY-HI-YA-HEY

HEY-HI-YA-HO

—prayer song taught to me by my adopted brother Dale Awasis from
Thunderchild First Nation, Saskatchewan

â-haw, ni-châpanak Charlotte,   *an invocation, my ancestral grandmothers*
Sarah, Mary ekwa Christiana.

â-haw,

kayâs ochi nikâwîmahk   *my mothers of long ago*

natohta   *listen*
my song, nikamowin   *the song*

âw,
this song I am singing

to give you back the
polished swan bones,

the sewing awl, the birchbark bundle
holding the whetstone,

the drawing stone, the pounding
chokecherry stone, âw

the spirit of your iskwew   *woman*
names, the ones

not birthed from the belly
of their ships, not taken

from their manitowimasinahikan,   *bible*
âw, their great naming book

ni-châpanak Charlotte,   *my ancestral grandmothers*
Sarah, Mary

ekwa Christ-i-ana,   *and*
these are the names

I've thrown back across the water,
I've given back

to their God
who has two hearts, two tongues

to speak with.
âw, natohta   *listen*

my song, nikamowin   *the song*
the renaming song

I am singing
five generations later,

natohta   *listen*
my prayer song

so you will be called,
sung as:

Tattooed From The Lip To The Chin Woman,
êy-hey! Sung as:

She Paints Her Face With Red Ochre,
êy-hey! Sung as:

Charm Woman Who Is Good To Make A Nation
Woman, êy-hey!

I give you back
ni-châpanak

the names to name
the names of bones, oskana   *the bones*

you laid down
to build them a house, âw

the blood, mihko   *blood*
and warm skin

earth, askîy   *earth*
that built them an empire.

natohta   *listen*
my song, nikamowin   *the song*

the prayer song
I am singing

to bring back
your stolen sons

whose sons and sons
and their missing bones

are unsung geese
lost in a country

across the water
ni-châpanak   *my ancestral grandmothers*

I've thrown back
your names;

nâmoya kîyawaw   *you are not*
Charlotte, Sarah, Mary

ekwa Christiana.	*and*
nâmoya kîyawaw môniyaskwewak.	*you are not white women*
â-haw, ni-châpanak	*an invocation, my ancestral grandmothers*
kayâs ochi nikâwîmahk	*my mothers of long ago*
natohta	*listen*
my song, nikamowin	*the song*

this prayer song
I am singing.

êy-hey!

NOTE: My châpanak of five generations past and my mothers of long ago came to find me while I was researching my maternal genealogy. The meticulous records that the Hudson's Bay Company kept on their employees, now available in their archives, serve as an invaluable source of information for many Metis and half-breed people, especially those who originate from western Canada. My grandfathers of that era, many of whom came from the Orkneys and London, arrived in Canada in the mid- to late 1700s. Some of them, such as James Peter Whitford, landed at York Factory, one of the Company's principal posts. Records state his full name, the parish he belonged to in London, the date he entered service, his various appointments and positions, the dates of his postings and his death on May 5, 1818 at Red River Settlement. Below this information, it simply states: *Wife: Sarah, an Indian woman. Married pre-1795 at Severn(?) Buried 27 Apr. 1845, 70 years old, at Upper Church.* I am certain my châpan Sarah, my kayâs ochi nikâwî—who eventually gave birth to eight children—came to my ancestor/ grandfather carrying a name too sacred for him to pronounce. During my research I began to talk to her in a language that caused her bones to shift beneath the earth. I asked her to help me, her little ni-châpanis, to find and sing the proper names, even though the old names are forever lost. The women of my blood, my other châpanak, came to listen. I was grateful to have made this connection, to be part of a ceremony that cannot be recorded.

THIS IS MY BLANKET

"An Indian and his blanket were inseparable."

—Barry Friedman, *Country Home Magazine* (October, 2008)

I am nothing without my blanket.
This is the key to the storehouse.
I am in charge here.

This is my blanket,
spectacularly hued, wildly patterned.
An end to the Indian wars.

I am federally licensed to write this poem.
I am nothing without my blanket.
This is the big aha of the whole thing.

This is the key to the storehouse,
brimming with treasure.
Hail the missing and murdered,

the names yet recorded. I am in charge here.
It's not that I am a country wife to be swooned.
It's not that straightforward.

I wear this blanket to keep my mother warm.
She lived in a meat truck
made homey with doilies and rag-rugs.

Each month she cashed her cheque
because she was federally licensed to.
This is the big aha of the whole thing.

She was nothing without her blanket,
my mama, the Perpetual Lady of Sorrows.
But this is not to say

she was easily swooned.
She wore her blanket like perfume.
It was her formal dress, a real zinger.

I am nothing without my blanket.
This is the key to my aunty's house.
She got raped here.
On this blanket
spectacularly hued, wildly patterned.
An end to the Indian wars.

The man who did it
was federally licensed.
Now her blanket is a living, breathing textile,

not something you fish out of the closet
when it stops snowing.
This is the big aha of the whole thing.

This is my blanket.
This is the key to the storehouse.
I am in charge here.

Halfbreed Heaven must be
handmade flowers of tissue,
poplar trees
forever in bloom,

the North and South Saskatchewan rivers
swirling and meeting
like the skirts, the hands
of cloggers
shuffling their moccasined feet.

I've been told

Halfbreed Heaven must be
old Gabriel at the gate
calling, "Tawow! Tawow!"   *Come in, you are welcome!*
toasting new arrivals, pointing
deportees
to the buffalo jump
or down the Great Canadian Railroad,
like Selkirk or MacDonald.

I've been told

Halfbreed Heaven must be
scuffed floors and furniture
pushed to one side,
grannies giggling in the kitchen,
their embroidered hankies
teasing and nudging
the sweetest sweet sixteen,
who will snare the eye
of the best jigger.

I've been told

Halfbreed Heaven must be
a wedding party
stretched to the new year,
into a wake, a funeral
then another wedding,
an endless brigade of happy faces
in squeaky-wheeled carts
loaded with accordions, guitars
and fiddles.

I've been told

Halfbreed Heaven must be
a rest-over for the Greats:
Hank Williams, Kitty Wells,
The Carter Family
and Hank Snow.

It must be
because I've been told so,

because I know
two Metis women who sing
beyond the blue.

Who didn't know my aunty

This story is told in oral traditional in a voice much older than mine, a voice whose thought process and first language is Cree. The story, though written in English, is a translation. I've heard old people speak in both Cree and English many times and I am immediately drawn into their rhythms, the poetry of their voices.

a few years ago   at a reading
of erotic poetry
a poet read a poem
by another poet
about a toothless Eskimo woman
in a bar
looking for someone, anyone
to buy her a drink   and
what she did, what
that Eskimo woman did for a drink

—

Long ago when my aunty was no longer Mean Man's wife—
Punching Bag Woman she was called—she had met a moniyâw, a
white man. He was the one who called her Good Cooking Day
Woman, or Good Laundry Day Woman, or sometimes, Good With
The Money Day Woman.

Now, my aunty had TB in her lungs—which took her from Edmonton
down to a hospital in Vancouver. I used to hear about it at that time; it
must have been hard for her.

She had three sons, my aunty did. But two of her boys got sick and
died in Wabasca. Her other boy, John Houle he was called, was killed
in a car accident coming home for Christmas. I used to hear

her talk about it sometimes. She'd say to me, *One night back home I was sitting having tea and I looked out at the clothesline and sure enough there were three owls sitting there, just sitting there hooting away on my clothesline. It's true,* she told me. *And those owls, those owls started making somersaults, spinning around and around like this,* she told me.

a few years ago   at a reading
of erotic poetry
a poet read a poem
by another poet
about a toothless Eskimo woman

who could be:

ni-châpan, Hunting To Feed The Family Woman   *my great-great-grandmother*

who could be:

ni-mâmâ, Holding Up The Walls Woman   *my mother*

who could be:

a kaskitewiyas-iskwew,   *a black woman*

sekipatwâw-iskwew,   *a Chinese woman*

moniyâw-iskwew   *a white woman*

running from a white man,
any man
into the arms of a poet

in a bar
looking for someone, anyone
to buy her a drink

—

My aunty, as I was saying here before, lost her boys early on.
That is how I came to be her son: "nikosis, now you take the place
of my John," she used to say. And I treated her as my mother:
ni-mâmâsis, my little mother, I used to call her. My own mother
—Dorothy was her name—did not mind this arrangement, for
it was good for me to have two mothers.

It was these women who raised me by themselves. They were poor,
my mothers, but it did not seem to matter—there were many
things to keep a young boy occupied: books, music, stories and
beadwork. I recall one time watching my aunty sew some moccasins.
So interested was I that I kept moving closer and closer to
her work. She did not seem to mind this...Now, my little mother
used to sew with very long threads and her needle would move
very quickly. But this time I did not pay attention, so engrossed
with the moccasins was I. She must have known this, for she took
her sâponikan, that needle, and poked me right on the nose. *awas,
ma-kôt!* She said. *Go on, big nose!* That is what she told me.

—

a few years ago   at a reading
of erotic poetry
a poet read a poem
by another poet
about a toothless Eskimo woman

she was fat, a seal
for the taking

she was dirty, a bag
of muskox bones
crawling with lice

she was dumb, her language
click, click
made people laugh

she was looking
for someone, anyone
to buy her a drink

—

I will not say my mothers did not have trouble with drinking or
they did not lose days keeping the house in order. It is true: they
had weaknesses here and there, just like other people.

And as far as my little mother goes, though she loved me a great
deal, she did not get over losing her boys. I guess that is why today
I speak so proudly of her, for she taught me many good things.

—

A few years ago   at a reading
of erotic poetry
a poet read a poem
by another poet
about a toothless Eskimo woman

and what she did   that woman
did for a drink.

It was in a bar:

it could be
the one from my childhood,

a room of white faces, a poetry hall
of uproarious mouths,

a room of unbound limbs
laughing
deep in their bones

or it could be
my aunty's rape bed, the man
who took her like a monument,
step after violent step

or it could be
her deathbed, all sixty-nine years
of her
lost in the translation
of a policeman's report

it could be, yes
the bed
where she, told me stories

â-ha, the bed
where I laid dreaming

—

This is as much as I am able to tell about my aunty. But there is
another thing, one more thing you should know: I loved her very
much and I still think of her whenever I am lonesome. ekosi,
I am done.

KIM THÚY is a well-regarded figure in both French and English Canadian letters. She was born in Saigon, Vietnam, in 1968. She grew up in Vietnam until the age of ten when she, her parents, and her two brothers fled the country's communist regime. As refugees of the Vietnam War they were known as "Boat People," and their mass flight led to an international humanitarian crisis. Her family spent time in a Malaysian refugee camp before arriving in Granby, Québec, and settling in Longueuil, a suburb of Montréal. As she grew up in Montréal, Thúy dabbled in a number of professions, from seamstress to cook, before attending the Université de Montréal, where she received a degree in linguistics and translation and another in law. After graduation, Thúy once again engaged in a number of diverse careers, including lawyer, translator, interpreter, and Montréal restaurateur, opening a restaurant that introduced Montréal to Vietnamese cuisine. Thúy began to write after her restaurant (named Ru de Nam) closed, and her work was instantly received with excitement. She published her first novel, *Ru* (Libre Expression), in 2009, which met critical acclaim and bestseller status in Québec. *Ru* engages with ideas of cultural identity, survival, and family, borrowing loosely from Thúy's own life. In 2010, *Ru* was published in France (Liana Levi) and won the Grand Prix TRL-Lire at the Salon du livre in Paris. Back in Canada, *Ru* won the

2010 Governor General's Award for French-language fiction. Beautifully translated into English by Sheila Fischman (Random House Canada, 2012), *Ru* was shortlisted for the 2012 Scotiabank Giller Prize and the 2013 Amazon.ca First Novel Award. It was also the winner of CBC Radio One's 2015 Canada Reads competition and was defended by Toronto International Film Festival Director Cameron Bailey. Thúy's next publication was *À toi* (Libre Expression, 2011), an epistolary collaboration between Thúy and Franco-Slovakian writer Pascal Janovjak, wherein the two share their online correspondence, exploring such themes as writing, language, and memory. Thúy's second novel, *Mãn* (Libre Expression, 2013), was also well-received and translated into English again by Fischman (Random House Canada, 2014). *Mãn* tells the story of a woman who emigrates from Vietnam to join a Vietnamese restaurateur in Montréal and, while cooking and combining flavours of her home with those of Québec and North America, begins to combine Vietnamese ways of life with those of her new country. Today Thúy continues to live and work in Montréal. She visited the Canadian Literature Centre for her Brown Bag Lunch reading on February 12, 2014.

10

KIM THÚY

A Gentle Power

PAMELA V. SING

IN 2009, thirty-one years after fleeing her homeland as a ten-year-old child and one of countless thousands of Vietnam's "Boat People," Kim Thúy published her first novel, *Ru*. She suddenly found herself poised to become one of Canada's most well-known and sought-after francophone writers. This slim volume of poetic prose is divided into 114 vignettes or fragments, each between four lines and three pages long. It recounts the journey of a young privileged citizen of Vietnam, whom war transforms into a dispossessed and displaced individual. *Ru*'s girl protagonist must survive life in a Malaysian refugee camp before taking up the challenge of starting life anew in Québec. *À toi* follows *Ru* and is an epistolary exchange composed of 109 similarly short texts, each between one and a half lines and two and a half pages long. As for Thúy's second short novel, *Mãn*, it is composed of ninety-nine fragments, each between eight lines and three pages long. The young Vietnamese woman featured in this novel is subjected to an arranged marriage that relocates her to Québec, where her search for fulfillment leads her to discover new ways of engaging with the world. Taken together, these three works reveal the main thematic categories in Thúy's writing: social and familial relationships (with a marked emphasis on women's roles, burdens, and sacrifice); geosocial and cultural displacement; multiple states of belonging; and survival, memory, writing, and language issues.

The fact that Thúy has become an important Canadian writer in such a short time certainly indicates the interest that "migrant literature" continues to generate in the country. Indeed, the term *écriture migrante*, coined by Robert Berrouët-Oriol in the Montréal magazine *Vice versa* in 1986, became an emblematic marker for Québec literature when Pierre Nepveu used it in his seminal 1988 volume, *L'Écologie du réel: Mort et naissance de la littérature québécoise contemporaine*. Nepveu emphasized his preference for *migrante* rather than *immigrante*; his interest concerned a literature less based on the experience and reality of immigration, than defined in terms of a poetics capable of expressing aspects of immigrant and exilic experiences, such as movement, drifting, and different kinds of intermingling. More importantly, Thúy's success is due more to *how* she writes about exile than to the fact that exile is at the heart of her writing.

The short prose form that has become Thúy's trademark constitutes a particularly effective mode of writing for the experiences she shares with her readers. The fragment and its inherent ruptures are markers for a feeling of psychological "disintegration" experienced by the displaced person. No longer able to identify wholly with one culture, her "in-betweenness" becomes a defining trait. Moreover, the use of fragment is suggestive of life narrative itself as testimony, of that which is both preserved and unfinished. It is therefore a particularly apt form for dealing with topics such as memory processes, the construction of the past, and the discovery that the meaning attributed to a given incident or action changes with time.

Ru charts the journey that takes its protagonist and first-person narrator, Nguyễn An Tịnh, from Saigon, where her family led privileged lives, to the Malaysian refugee camp where they spent four harrowing months. They then arrive in the Québec town of Granby, whose citizens welcome them and fellow refugees with open arms and hearts, eager to help them settle into their new life. When, years later, the narrator returns to Vietnam as an adult, she learns which aspects of her cultural identity have continued to be shaped by the childhood spent in her former homeland, and which ones confirm her Canadianness.

The narrative of what could be considered as the four "chapters" of the narrator's story eschews linear, chronological order, and adopts instead a structure dependent on word, image, and sentient associations. In this way, the text mimics the manner in which thoughts occur and memory functions. Following the logic of mnemonic and thought processes, the story oscillates between the present and the past, and shifts back and forth between Vietnam, Malaysia, and Québec, as well as between tales concerning the narrator, her ancestors, members of her immediate and extended family, friends, acquaintances, or even individuals encountered only in passing.

One has the impression that Thúy conceives of a theme in the form of clusters or bundles of related details whose interconnections are revealed as the narrative unfolds, one layer at a time, so gently, that the reader remains unsuspecting of what lies at the heart of that bundle until the last line of the fragment is read. The analysis of the excerpts included in this anthology using a close-reading approach grounded in reception theory, which defines literature as the process of how the reader and the text interact with each other, can help to elucidate Thúy's writing practice.

The first half of the excerpts from *Ru* cited in this anthology—which are from the novel's sixty-fourth, sixty-sixth, and sixty-seventh fragments— begins on a reassuring, positive note. The possibility of anyone realizing *"le rêve américain"* encapsulates the promise that the New World represents for people in many parts of the globe. In *Ru*, it bodes well that the American dream comes true for many, and particularly for one couple who has experienced the dreadful conditions of the refugee camp and now can share its good fortune with the entire family. Indeed, the dysphoria associated with the camps appears to be a thing of the distant past. Little by little, however, the fragment segues into revelations of the darker consequences of "dreaming American." First, An Tịnh, *Ru*'s narrator, asserts that her *tante* and *bel-oncle Six*'s wealthier existence has meant that family gatherings have lost their former intensity and reassuring closeness. No sooner does the reader begin to assimilate the meaning of this seemingly nostalgic valorization of the recent past when the narrator reveals that part of the social glue that had held them together was the shared difficulty of starting a new life in a world where their only point of reference was initially a shared, vague, seemingly impossible "dream." When that dream becomes a personal reality for An Tịnh, she discovers an even greater loss—that of her membership to Vietnamese society. And just as she becomes aware of that truth, she learns that she will never be considered a full-fledged member of Québécois society either.

Thúy thus deals with the American dream as the key element of a network of incidents and developments, each of which belongs to different people, places, and time periods and is associated with a particular sensation, sentiment, or meaning. She produces a multi-layered, subjective, intimate, and organic telling of exilic experience, which enables us to appreciate its complexity. Her narrator chooses to embrace her in-betweenness by "loving everyone without belonging to anyone": "J'ai choisi de les aimer tous, sans appartenir à aucun" (88). Here, she indicates her acknowledgement of others, regardless of their culture, and her acceptance of all attempts to define her. In other words, her openness transcends the traditional tendency to see oneself as having a fixed or reducible cultural identity. In effect, An Tịnh claims to be as receptive to the man from the small Saguenay town of Saint-Félicien, who assumes she does not understand French, as she is to the rickshaw-cyclist in Danang, who mistakes her for her husband's escort, or to the Hanoian woman, a tofu street vendor, who takes her for a Japanese woman learning Vietnamese.

The memory of this last misidentification leads to the question of language, a theme that allows An Tịnh to establish connections between her own linguistic identity and that of each of her two homelands. She does so by first explaining why she has effectively needed to re-learn her mother tongue. Having left Vietnam at such a young age, not only is her mastery of Vietnamese incomplete, but also, at the time, Vietnam had two native languages, and the speakers of one were unfamiliar with the idiom of the other. Emphasizing that like Canada, Vietnam was a country of two solitudes, each with a language that evolved in relation to specific sociocultural and political circumstances, An Tịnh goes on to illustrate her point through the choice of three categories of new words. In North Vietnam, all three are associated with war, whereas in American-friendly South Vietnam, where new realities were more diverse, so also were the words needed to name those realities. Typically, her first example refers to a pleasant, intimate reality easily recognized by almost every reader in the world—the global "all-American" feeling of Coca-Cola's effervescence on one's tongue; she follows it with the category of words needed to identify the enemy, that is to say the anti-American *espions*, *rebelles*, and *sympathisants communistes dans les rues du sud* who sought to overthrow South Vietnam's government. Just as the reader is about to conclude that life was better in South Vietnam than in its northern counterpart thanks in large part to the Americans, An Tịnh reveals that a third category of new words was needed to name the scores of children born to the Vietnamese women that the GIs (American soldiers) had impregnated during their nights of wild partying. Thúy ends the fragment without saying anything of the stigma attached to those young women and their mixed blood children. But the large portion of the page that remains blank intimates that much has (at least so far) been left unsaid. Subsequent fragments give us glimpses of the fate of both the providers of "paid love" and their progeny, and reflect other examples of the exploitation of women's bodies especially, but certainly not exclusively, in times of war. Young and perfect, these bodies bear the "invisible burden of Vietnam's history": "le poids invisible de l'histoire du Vietnam" (131).

This last point, which points to Thúy's delicate way of approaching sensitive or difficult themes, is crucial to understanding the appeal and power of all three of the literary works she has published so far. Thúy does not forget the dark moments integral to war and migrant experiences, but aims chiefly at building bridges between her native and new homelands. In *Ru*, this is suggested right at the outset, by the epigraph, which explains the signification of the novel's title both in French and in Vietnamese: En français, *ru* signifie « petit ruisseau » et, au figuré, « écoulement (de larmes, de sang, d'argent) » (*Le Robert historique*). En vietnamien, *ru* signifie « berceuse », « bercer ». ("In French, *ru* means a small stream and, figuratively, a flow, a discharge— of tears, of blood, of money. In Vietnamese, *ru* means a lullaby, to lull" [trans. Fischman n.p.]). Thereafter, allusions to the title or to one of its meanings appear throughout the novel, sometimes in relation to Vietnam, sometimes in relation to Québec. *Mãn* similarly expresses its bilingual and bicultural intent by prefacing each fragment with a word that suggests or summarizes the theme of that fragment, while also suggesting the complexity of the endeavour. If, for example, the "chapter" title "*muối* / sel" (43; "*muối* / salt") appears straightforward and therefore suggests cultural commonality, such is not the case for "*tiễn đưa* / dire adieu, accompagner quelqu'un jusqu'au point de son depart" (52; "*tiễn đưa* / to say goodbye, to accompany someone to the point of their departure"). By identifying different kinds of connections between her two homelands, Thúy accomplishes two main objectives. First, she reveals the multiple facets and flows of life characterizing Vietnamese history, culture, and society, the recognition of which discourages the consideration of immigrants in reductive ways. Second, she pays tribute to the society and culture that allowed a child refugee, who arrived in Québec bereft of the material means and knowledge necessary for survival, not only to become a successful writer or chef, but above all, to come to feel at home in that part of the globe. The second half of the excerpt included in this anthology, consisting of fragments eighty-nine to ninety-one of *Ru*, speaks in sensorial terms to the theme of Québec/Canada as home by focusing on the tactile aspects of life in Vietnam and in Québec. It underscores how the everyday smell of a North American fabric softener triggers the realization that, for all her sociocultural and linguistic hybridity, Thúy's narrator is unequivocally and affectively grounded in North America.

In one of *Ru*'s last fragments, An Tịnh refers ostensibly to her behaviour when seated in a bar. More significantly, the passage summarizes the approach adopted by the writer and public figure that Thúy herself has become:

[J]'ose me mettre à nu auprès d'amis, et parfois d'inconnus, à leur insu. Je leur raconte des bribes de mon passé comme si elles étaient des historiettes, des numéros d'humoriste ou des contes cocasses de pays lointains aux décors exotiques, aux sons insolites, aux personnages parodiques. (141)

(I dare to strip naked in front of friends and sometimes strangers, without their knowledge. I recount bits of my past as if they were anecdotes or comedy routines or amusing tales from far-off lands featuring exotic landscapes, odd sound effects and exaggerated characterizations.) (trans. Fischman 136)

Indeed, whether focusing on social and familial relationships, issues connected to geosocial and cultural dislocation, questions and techniques of survival, memory, writing, or language, the 114 vignettes that make up *Ru* introduce readers to the intimate dimensions of Vietnam's history and a female protagonist's migrant experience. The description of events in the form of clusters allows Thúy to reveal their multifarious aspects, while revelations of personal secrets, memories, or truths, some tender, others raw and painful, allow the reader to also feel them. Always, the choice of a poetic, lyrical prose and a lightness in tone suggest a non-judgemental voice and connote forgiveness, understanding, and humour. The reader is thus willingly led through the intricate web of human actions that make up both the small history of individual lives and the large history of a people. Even when the last line of a fragment reveals details such as the death of the woman who falls into the family cesspit, or the anguish of Mr. An, permanently traumatized since having a gun held against his temple and hearing the "click" of the trigger, Thúy makes it clear that for her narrator, the universe where such atrocities take place also contains much beauty, grace, and love.

Works Cited

Nepveu, Pierre. *L'Écologie du réel: Mort et naissance de la littérature québécoise contemporaine*. Montréal: Boréal, 1988. Print.

Thúy, Kim. *Mãn*. Montréal: Libre Expression, 2013. Print.

———. *Ru*. Montréal: Libre Expression, 2010. Print.

———. *Ru*. Trans. Sheila Fischman. Toronto: Vintage Canada, 2015. Print.

Ru (excerpt)

BEAUCOUP D'IMMIGRANTS ont réalisé le rêve américain. Il y a trente ans, peu importait la ville, que ce fût Washington DC, Québec, Boston, Rimouski ou Toronto, nous traversions des quartiers entiers parsemés de jardins de roses, de grands arbres centenaires, de maisons en pierre, mais l'adresse que nous cherchions ne figurait jamais sur l'une de ces portes. Aujourd'hui, ma tante Six et son mari (bel-oncle Six) habitent dans une de ces maisons. Ils voyagent en première classe et doivent coller un papier sur le dossier de leur siège pour que les hôtesses cessent de leur offrir des chocolats et du champagne. Il y a trente ans, dans notre camp de réfugiés en Malaisie, ce même bel-oncle Six rampait moins vite que sa fille de huit mois parce qu'il souffrait de carences alimentaires. Cette même tante Six devait coudre avec une seule aiguille des habits pour acheter du lait à sa fille. Il y a trente ans, nous vivions avec eux dans la noirceur, sans électricité, sans eau courante, sans intimité. Aujourd'hui, nous nous plaignons que leur maison est trop grande, et notre famille étendue, trop petite pour retrouver l'intensité qui habitait nos fêtes — jusqu'au petit matin — quand nous nous réunissions chez mes parents durant nos premières années en Amérique du Nord.

Nous étions vingt-cinq, parfois trente personnes, arrivant à Montréal de Fanwood, de Montpelier, de Springfield, de Guelph, réunies dans un petit appartement de trois chambres pendant tout le congé de Noël. Si quelqu'un voulait dormir seul, il fallait qu'il s'installe dans la baignoire. Autrement, nous étions tous les uns à côté des autres. Inévitablement, les discussions, les rires et les querelles duraient toute la nuit.

Chaque cadeau que nous nous offrions était réellement un cadeau car il n'était jamais futile. En fait, chaque cadeau était réellement un cadeau puisqu'il provenait d'abord et avant tout d'un sacrifice et était la réponse à un besoin, à un désir ou à un rêve. Nous connaissions bien les rêves de nos proches : nous étions serrés les uns contre les autres pendant des nuits entières. En ces temps-là, nous avions tous les mêmes rêves. Pendant longtemps, nous avons été obligés d'avoir les mêmes rêves, ceux du rêve américain.

—

CEPENDANT, UNE FOIS OBTENU, le rêve américain ne nous quitte plus, comme une greffe, ou une excroissance. La première fois que je suis allée avec mes talons hauts, ma jupe droite et mon porte-documents dans un restaurant-école pour enfants défavorisés à Hanoi, le jeune serveur de ma table n'a pas compris pourquoi je lui parlais en vietnamien. Je croyais au début qu'il ne saisissait pas mon accent du Sud. Mais, à la fin du repas, il m'a dit candidement que j'étais trop grosse pour être une Vietnamienne.

J'ai traduit cette remarque à mes patrons, qui en rient encore aujourd'hui. J'ai compris plus tard qu'il ne parlait pas de mes quarante-cinq kilos, mais de ce rêve américain qui m'avait épaissie, empâtée, alourdie. Ce rêve américain a donné de l'assurance à ma voix, de la détermination à mes gestes, de la précision à mes désirs, de la vitesse à ma démarche et de la force à mon regard. Ce rêve américain m'a fait croire que je pouvais tout avoir, que je pouvais me déplacer en voiture avec chauffeur et, en même temps, mesurer le poids des courges transportées sur une

190

Ten Canadian Writers in Context

bicyclette rouillée par une femme aux yeux brouillés par la sueur ; que je pouvais danser au même rythme que les filles qui se déhanchaient au bar pour étourdir les hommes aux portefeuilles bien garnis de dollars américains ; que je pouvais vivre dans ma grande villa d'expatriée et accompagner les enfants aux pieds nus jusqu'à leur école installée directement sur le trottoir, à l'intersection de deux rues.

Mais ce jeune serveur m'a rappelé que je ne pouvais tout avoir, que je n'avais plus le droit de me proclamer vietnamienne parce que j'avais perdu leur fragilité, leur incertitude, leurs peurs. Et il avait raison de me reprendre.

—

À LA MÊME ÉPOQUE, mon patron a découpé dans un journal montréalais un article qui réitérait que la « nation québécoise » était caucasienne, que mes yeux bridés me classaient automatiquement dans une catégorie à part même si le Québec m'avait donné mon rêve américain, même s'il m'avait bercée pendant trente ans. Alors, qui aimer? Personne ou chacun? J'ai choisi de les aimer tous, sans appartenir à aucun. J'ai décidé d'aimer le monsieur de Saint-Félicien qui m'a demandé en anglais de lui accorder une danse. « Follow the guy », m'a-t-il dit. J'aime aussi le cyclo-pousseur de Danang qui m'a demandé combien j'étais payée en tant qu'escorte de mon mari « blanc ». Et puis, je pense souvent à la vendeuse de tofu à cinq cents le morceau, assise par terre dans un coin caché du marché à Hanoi, qui racontait à ses voisines que j'étais japonaise, que mon vietnamien progressait rapidement.

Elle avait raison. J'ai dû réapprendre ma langue maternelle, que j'avais abandonnée trop tôt. De toute manière, je ne l'avais pas vraiment maîtrisée de façon complète parce que le pays était divisé en deux quand je suis née. Je viens de Sud, alors je n'avais jamais entendu les gens du Nord avant mon retour au pays. De même, les gens du Nord n'avaient jamais entendu les gens du Sud avant la réunification. Comme au

Canada, le Vietnam avait aussi ses deux solitudes. La langue du nord du Vietnam avait évolué selon sa situation politique, sociale et économique du moment, avec des mots pour décrire comment faire tomber un avion à l'aide d'une mitraillette installée sur un toit, comment accélérer la coagulation du sang avec du glutamate monosodique, comment repérer les abris quand les sirènes sonnent. Pendant ce temps, la langue du sud avait créé des mots pour exprimer la sensation des bulles du Coca-Cola sur la langue, des termes pour nommer les espions, les rebelles, les sympathisants communistes dans les rues du sud, des noms pour désigner les enfants nés des nuits endiablées des GI.

—

J'AI DÉCOUVERT mon point d'ancrage quand je suis allée accueillir Guillaume à l'aéroport de Hanoi. Le parfum de l'assouplissant Bounce de son t-shirt m'a fait pleurer. Pendant quatorze jours, j'ai dormi avec un vêtement de Guillaume sur mon oreiller. Guillaume, de son côté, était ébloui par le parfum des jacquiers, des ramboutans, des kumquats, des durians, des caramboles, des courges amères, des crabes des champs, des crevettes séchées, des lis, des lotus, des herbes. Il est allé à plusieurs reprises au marché de nuit où des légumes, des fruits, des fleurs s'échangeaient entre les paniers des marchands, qui négociaient entre eux dans un chaos bruyant et contrôlé comme sur un plancher de Bourse. J'accompagnais Guillaume dans ce marché de nuit toujours avec un de ses pulls par-dessus ma chemise parce que j'avais découvert que mon chez-moi se résumait à cette odeur ordinaire, simple, banale du quotidien nord-américain. Je n'avais pas d'adresse civique à moi nulle part, je vivais dans un appartement du bureau à Hanoi. Mes livres étaient entreposés chez tante Huit, mes diplômes chez mes parents à Montréal, mes photos chez mes frères, mes manteaux d'hiver chez mon ancienne colocataire. J'ai constaté pour la première fois que le Bounce, l'odeur du Bounce, m'avait donné mon premier mal du pays.

PENDANT MES PREMIÈRES années au Québec, mes vêtements sentaient l'humidité ou la nourriture parce que, après le lavage, ils étaient accrochés dans nos chambres sur des cordes tendues entre deux murs. La nuit, toutes les nuits, ma dernière image a été des couleurs suspendues à travers la chambre comme les drapeaux de prière tibétains. Pendant des années, j'ai respiré le parfum d'assouplissant des vêtements de mes camarades de classe quand un vent le transportait jusqu'à moi. Je humais avec bonheur les sacs de vêtements usagés que nous recevions. Je ne désirais que cette odeur.

GUILLAUME EST REPARTI après son séjour de deux semaines à Hanoi avec moi. Il n'avait plus aucun vêtement propre à me laisser. Au cours des mois suivants, j'ai reçu par la poste de temps à autre un mouchoir fraîchement séché au Bounce dans un sac de plastique hermétiquement fermé. Le dernier paquet qu'il m'a envoyé contenait un billet d'avion pour Paris. Il m'y attendait pour un rendez-vous chez un parfumeur. Il voulait que je sente la feuille de violette, l'iris, le cyprès bleu, la vanilline, la livèche...et surtout l'immortelle, une odeur à propos de laquelle Napoléon disait qu'il pouvait sentir son pays avant même d'y avoir posé le pied. Guillaume voulait que je trouve une odeur qui me donnerait mon pays, mon univers.

Essay Contributors

MARIE CARRIÈRE is Director of the Canadian Literature Centre/
Centre de littérature canadienne at the University of Alberta,
where she also teaches Canadian literature in English and French.
She is the author of *Médée protéiforme* (University of Ottawa
Press, 2012) and co-editor of *Regenerations/Régénérations: Canadian
Women's Writing/Écriture des femmes au Canada* with Patricia Demers
(University of Alberta Press, 2014). With a new book in view, her
current research focuses on the work of Canadian, Québécois, and
Indigenous women writers, the language of crisis, metafeminism,
and the ethics of care.

JENNIFER BOWERING DELISLE is the author of *The Newfoundland
Diaspora: Mapping the Literature of Out-Migration* (Wilfrid Laurier
University Press, 2013) and numerous articles on Canadian lit-
erature. She has held postdoctoral fellowships at the University
of Alberta and McMaster University, and is now the Lead
Instructional Designer for Yardstick Testing and Training. *The
Bosun Chair*, a hybrid of family memoir and poetry, is forthcoming
from NeWest Press.

KIT DOBSON is an Associate Professor of English at Mount Royal
University. His research looks at Canadian literature, film, and
culture, with a particular focus on questions of globality, dias-
pora, Indigeneity, and social justice. Recent books include
Transnationalism, Activism, Art (University of Toronto Press, 2013;
co-edited with Áine McGlynn) and *Producing Canadian Literature:
Authors Speak on the Literary Marketplace* (Wilfrid Laurier University
Press, 2013; with Smaro Kamboureli). He is at work on a book about
shopping in Canada.

CURTIS GILLESPIE has written five books and won seven National
Magazine Awards and is co-founder and editor of the award-
winning magazine *Eighteen Bridges*. Curtis has worked with many
writers through the University of Alberta, *Eighteen Bridges*, and
the Banff Centre (where he is co-founder and lead faculty of
Frontline) and has served as a volunteer with Litfest, the Nina
Haggerty Centre, the National Magazine Awards Foundation, and
the Canadian Literature Centre. Curtis received the University of
Alberta's Alumni Honour Award in 2014, the Edmonton Artist's
Trust Fund Award in 2015, and was named Alberta Magazine
Publishers Association Editor of the Year in 2016.

DANIEL LAFOREST is Associate Professor at the University of Alberta,
where he teaches Québec and French literature, cultural stud-
ies, and critical theory. He has been Fulbright Fellow at the Centre
for Cultural Studies of the University of California, Santa Cruz;
holder of the Chair in Canadian Studies of the Universités de
Limoges and Poitiers in France; and Visiting Professor at Stanford
University. He serves as associate editor for the journal *Canadian
Literature/Littérature canadienne*. He has released two monographs:
L'Archipel de Caïn: Pierre Perrault et l'écriture du territoire (XYZ, 2010),
and *L'Âge de plastique: Lire la ville contemporaine au Québec* (Presses de
l'Université de Montréal, 2016).

DON PERKINS is a Faculty Lecturer in the Department of English and Film Studies at the University of Alberta. He has taught courses in Canadian drama, Canadian literature of the late twentieth century, popular culture, Aboriginal literature, and creative non-fiction writing, as well as a course called "Reading the Local." He is co-editor of *Intersections: Readings in the Sciences and Humanities* (Pearson, 2004). He is currently on the board of the Edmonton Poetry Festival, with recent poems published in *40 Below: Edmonton's Winter Anthology* (Wufniks Press, 2013) and *The Trumpeter* (2014), and performed at the 2015 Edmonton Poetry Festival.

JOSEPH PIVATO is Professor Emeritus of literary studies at Athabasca University in Edmonton. He has published ten books on ethnic minority writing, comparative literature, Italian-Canadian literature and on these authors: Sheila Watson, George Elliott Clarke, Mary di Michele, Caterina Edwards, F.G. Paci, Pier Giorgio DiCicco, and Rina Del Nin Cralli.

JASON PURCELL is a graduate student at the University of Alberta in the Department of English and Film Studies. He is the Communications Officer for the Canadian Literature Centre/ Centre de littérature canadienne at the University of Alberta, the Circulation Coordinator for *Eighteen Bridges* magazine, and the Manuscript Coordinator at NeWest Press.

JULIE RODGERS is a Lecturer in French at Maynooth University, Ireland, and is preparing a monograph examining maternal counternarratives in contemporary women's writing and film in French. Julie has published three articles on Ying Chen to date: in *Dialogues francophones* (2011), the *International Journal of Canadian Studies* (2012), and a special issue of *Québec Studies* (2015). A chapter contribution focusing on Chen is forthcoming in *Starvation, Food Obsessions and Identity: Eating Disorders in Post-1968 Women's Writing*, edited by Petra Bagley, Francesca Calamita, and Kathryn Robson

(Peter Lang, 2016). Julie is currently secretary of the Association of Canadian Studies in Ireland.

WINFRIED SIEMERLING is Professor of English at the University of Waterloo and an Associate of the W.E.B. Du Bois Institute at Harvard University. His most recent monograph is *The Black Atlantic Reconsidered: Black Canadian Writing, Cultural History, and the Presence of the Past* (McGill-Queen's University Press, 2015). Earlier books include *Canada and Its Americas* (McGill-Queen's University Press, 2010, co-ed.), *The New North American Studies* (Routledge, 2005, French trans., 2010), and *Discoveries of the Other* (University of Toronto Press, 1994). He has contributed chapters to *The Oxford Handbook of the African American Slave Narrative* (Oxford University Press, 2014) and *The Cambridge History of Postcolonial Literature* (Cambridge University Press, 2012).

PAMELA V. SING is Director of the Institut d'études canadiennes/ Institute of Canadian Studies at Campus Saint-Jean, the University of Alberta's francophone campus, and Associate Director of the Canadian Literature Centre/Centre de littérature canadienne at the University of Alberta. She teaches French, Québec, and Franco-Canadian literature at Campus Saint-Jean and is the co-editor of *Impenser la francophonie: Recherches, renouvellement, diversité, identité* with Estelle Dansereau (Campus Saint-Jean, 2012). Her research focuses on Franco-Canadian and Québécois writers, as well as Canadian and American writers of Franco-Métis ancestry.

MAÏTÉ SNAUWAERT is Assistant Professor at the University of Alberta. Her research delves into literary discourses of the end of life, with a particular emphasis on mourning memoirs published in France, Québec, Canada, and the United States. She is the author of *Philippe Forest, la littérature à contretemps* (Nantes, Cécile Defaut, 2012) and of several articles on Canadian and French women writers (Annabel Lyon, Gabrielle Roy, Nicole Brossard, Catherine

Mavrikakis, Marguerite Duras, Annie Ernaux, Marie NDiaye, Jane Sautière, Sophie Calle).

ANGELA VAN ESSEN is a PHD candidate in the Department of English and Film Studies at the University of Alberta, where she is writing a dissertation on contemporary Cree bilingual litera-ture. She has taught English courses at the University of Alberta and Maskwacîs Cultural College and has published on Indigenous writers in Canada.

Permissions

Excerpt from *Le Mangeur* by Ying Chen. Copyright © 2006 Ying Chen. Reprinted by permission of Les Éditions du Boréal.

Excerpt from *L'Ingratitude* by Ying Chen. Copyright © 1995 Ying Chen. Reprinted by permission of Leméac Éditeur.

Excerpt from *The Antagonist* by Lynn Coady. Copyright © 2011 Lynn Coady. Reprinted by permission of House of Anansi Press Inc.

Excerpt from *Sweetland* by Michael Crummey. Copyright © 2014 Michael Crummey Ink. Reprinted by permission of Doubleday Canada, a division of Penguin Random House Canada Limited, A Penguin Random House Company.

Excerpt from *Finding Rosa* by Caterina Edwards. Copyright © 2008 Caterina Edwards. Reprinted by permission of Greystone Books.

Excerpt from *Close to Hugh* by Marina Endicott. Copyright © 2015 Marina Endicott. Reprinted by permission of Doubleday Canada, a division of Penguin Random House Canada Limited, A Penguin Random House Company.

Revised and abridged version of "Meet You at the Door," *The Walrus* (January/Feburary 2011) by Lawrence Hill. Copyright © 2011 Lawrence Hill. Reprinted by permission of Lawrence Hill Creative Services, Inc.

Excerpt from *The Office Tower Tales* by Alice Major. Copyright © 2008 Alice Major. Reprinted by permission of University of Alberta Press.

Excerpt from *The Sasquatch at Home: Traditional Protocols & Modern Storytelling* by Eden Robinson. Copyright © 2011 Eden Robinson. Reprinted by permission of University of Alberta Press.

"Prayer Song for the Returning of Names and Sons," "This Is My Blanket," "I've Been Told," and "Conversation with the Poet Who Didn't Know My Aunty," *Kipocihkân: Poems New & Selected* by Gregory Scofield. Copyright © 2009 Gregory Scofield. Reprinted by permission of Nightwood Editions.

Excerpts from *Ru* by Kim Thúy. Copyright © 2010 Kim Thúy. Reprinted by permission of Groupe Librex (Libre Expression).